What.

I0134240

More from Lionel Goulet

The Field, paperback and Kindle.
Search on Amazon for "The Field Lionel Goulet":
https://www.amazon.com/Field-story-about-future/dp/0615311172/

What.

A Better Image of God
by Lionel Goulet

What.

A Better Image of God

No part of this book may be reproduced, or stored in a retrieval system, or transmitted in any form or by any means, electronic, mechanical, photocopying, recording, or otherwise; without express written permission of the Copyright holder.

What. is neither free nor in the public domain.

Copyright © 2024 Lionel Goulet
All Rights Reserved

Second Edition, November, 2024.
Published previously with the subtitle *A New Image of God.*
Turns out it's not new, but it is better.

ISBN: 978-0-578-51701-8

Contact Lionel Goulet
QCO at Quiet Counsel dot org

If you should by any chance want to discuss stuff with me, send me an email.
I would really like hashing this out with you.

I would also like to say this book is meant to be *read* quietly, not read aloud. I've read it aloud to others a couple times. Nope.
It is not theatrical. It is not entertaining.
It is *way* too dense for casual listeners.
It needs to be *studied*. That's my writing style.
Too much in too few words. Sorry. Good luck.
Thanks for trying.

God is perfectly understandable.

Te Deum – Thou art God. *Divinus es* – You are divine.

All This is That.

that that is is that that is not is not is that it it is

Welcome all things.
Receive them as gifts.
Let yourself learn to love.

Thank you for this day, oh Lord.
The joys and the sorrows.
The loves and the fears.
The laughs and the pains.
Let me live it to the best. Amen.

May the sun bring you energy by day
May the moon softly restore you by night
May the rain wash away your worries
May the breeze blow new strength into your being
May you walk gently through the world and know its beauty
All the days of your life.

– Isabelle Perico Enjady

To Susan Lee, my source,
and Alex and Adam, my support squad.
And all the lessons you have taught me.
If I had it to do all over again, I wouldn't change a thing.

What's Where

0. Intro

This is what I believe. If I don't say that in front of every paragraph, *understand* it is there.

I love people. I love truth. I am an introvert. I have looked inside myself pretty-much all my life for the truth about me, the truth about people, the truth about truth. And slowly, over the decades, I have seen things, heard things, felt things. Of course, truth is an endless search, but *what I seen, man; what I seen*!

When I walk the streets, I want to help the people I see. People do not understand God, and when we don't understand God, we don't understand ourselves. Without even knowing it, we are cut off from our *source*. There is even a thread in human thinking that holds that God is beyond human understanding: God the *forbidden*; God the *mystery*.

What a shame. Big mistake. What a terrible *loss*. God is perfectly understandable. The reason God seems so beyond understanding is because we have piled enormous crud on God. That crud-coated pile is what we don't understand.

It is time to scrape off the crud.

I wonder if we coat God with crud on purpose maybe, to obscure God, to not have to confront God? Are we afraid to face God, to face the God-in-us? Humans have a lot of fear. Is that what's going on? If so, it's a terrible price to pay for something so easily fixed.

Humans have progressed in the thousands of years of recorded history; since the *Gita*, since the *Tao*, since the *Upanishads*, since the *Testaments*, since the *Qur'an*, since the *Small Catechism*, even since *Science and Health*. Everything about us is more sophisticated now. It's time for a 21st Century image of God. Amen.

-Lionel Goulet 14 May 2024 Waltham, MA

This Was the Original Intro

People do not worship God. People worship symbols of God. People worship images of God. People worship traditions. People worship tradition itself.
Sorry. It's not on purpose, but it's true.
People worship the Son of God, the Messenger of God, the Word of God, the Enlightened One… but, *God*? Not so much.

And they're so *emotional* about their symbols and images; *very* committed to them. Even people who worship *No God* do so angrily; at least, in my experience.
Again with the emotion!

I can understand this, I think.
We need to worship *something*, it's a fundamental human need, and something that we can see is easier to worship than something we can't see.

Except we can. See God, that is. Who told you you couldn't?

This is the 21st Century. We have conquered the atom. We are starting to know how the brain works. We internet. We know the importance of inter-connectedness and interdependence on a global scale.

We have become, very much, a sophisticated, *planetary* species. We can tell that is true by the size of our problems.

Why is "God" so tribal, so primitive, so *frightening*?

Why do we have to *please* God? Why does God get *angry* with us? Why does God *forgive* us? Why does God get happy, want, punish, reward, or *need* anything?

Such a God is not God, but a human in a God costume. God-Man; Super-Human, like, Spider-Man.

Each of us is a two-way path to the divine. Primitives thought that path was very long, God afar off; God in heaven.

No. Not at all.

God is close; very close indeed. Closer than those tiny little hairs on our skin. Closer than the air in our lungs.
Closer than that.
Thank God!

We want to know what we are.
We want to know what God is.
We want to know what it's all about.
We want to know *what*. Hence, the title of this book.

I've been thinking about this a lot; at least since I was 5.

I've been asking for the kind of enlightenment Jesus, the Buddha, Martin Luther, Saul of Tarsus, Mary Baker Eddy, John Wesley, Bill Wilson, and many others received. What I have discovered in that search for enlightenment is this: it doesn't only come suddenly; waking you up, warming you, descending upon you like a dove, a *flash* of light, a glimpse of heaven. It can also be incremental: one tiny thought at a time, almost unnoticed.

Life leaves us clues everywhere if you look for them.
If we look for them.

It's taken me *decades* to figure life out. Now that I've got it figured out and it makes sense to me, I wrote it down.
I want to share it. I hope to make it make sense to you too.

Many people reading this book will conclude it has something to do with religion. It does, but not in the way most people think. Religion is not a set of beliefs and rules and rituals and traditions, though it can be that. Religion at its core is an attempt to give *meaning* to our lives. The differences between religions, to me, are the different meanings they help us find. *What.* is a better meaning than the one we now have.

There are a whole lot of people who are afraid of God. The simple word "God" makes them uncomfortable, uneasy.
Be not afraid. God will not hurt you. God cannot hurt you. God has never hurt you, or anyone else; despite what you may think.

Let me bring up that word again: *meaning*. This book will help you change the meaning of your story. If you want to, that is. If you need to, that is.

When I say this book is "a better image of God," what I am trying to do is help us all find a better *relationship* with divinity; *our* divinity.

"God" is *our* God.

Not just new. Better.
I sincerely hope.

Note.

I couldn't afford to have this book professionally edited.

Do not be put off by my choppy, aggressive writing style: lots of ideas; few words.
I eschew obfuscation by sesquipedalianisms.

Also, watch my pronouns. Sometimes I use "we," sometimes I use "you," sometimes I use "our," sometimes I use "us."
Generally, I used the word I needed to use. For example:
>   "We are divine." Broad statement. Low power.
>   "You are divine." Pointed statement. High power.
Both are true.

One last thing.
The first four printings of this book were subtitled *A New Image of God*.

Turns out that wasn't even remotely correct.
The image of God in this book is not at all new.
It's been around a long, long time but it somehow got lost.
Not new. Maybe new to you; and better. Read on and see.

1. What We Are

Before we define God, we need to define us: human beings. This is because, well, just *because*. By the end of the next chapter this will make sense. Hang on. This part has to come first.

What we are is both really complicated and really simple. My definition of "human being" is not based on what seems to be. Be aware of that. We need to take a better look at ourselves. That's what makes it complicated.

But looking at ourselves with a new pair of eyes is something we do every new day. That's what makes it really simple. Here we go.

Try #1: The Colander and the Sacred[1]

> Did you hear the one about the student waiting for the bus in the rain who took out an umbrella and under-stood?

The popular image of "human being" is: a limited mortal body with a magic something-or-other inside of it. We are:
- body and soul
- mind and body
- a ghost in the machine
- the host of a divine spark.

---

[1] Tries 2 through 7 are in the back of the book, the *Endendum*.

Poetic? Yes.
Factual? No!
That's not it. No siree Bob!²

Here's a story to help illustrate what we really are. It's about a colander. You know, a bowl with a whole lot of holes in it that a cook will use to wash beans or pasta. Pay attention to the colander. It becomes important early in the story.

A friend of yours invites you over to their house for an evening. When you get there, you see your friend lives in a first-class home; a spectacular home. You knock on the front door and the butler lets you in.

> When choosing between two evils, I always like to try the one I've never tried before. -Mae West

The butler takes you to the library. It's a grand room with a high ceiling, books on all four walls, plush carpeting, two huge windows looking out into the gardens behind the house, a couch, and a small table. You enter.

On the table is a little lamp; a plain bare light bulb.

You sit down and kind-of admire everything. Very cool.
Except the light bulb, which looks totally out of place and very un-classy.

The light bulb illuminates the library room.
Bright, but not too bright.
Bright enough to look at it without hurting your eyes.

Just as you're getting used to it all, the butler comes into the library and covers the light bulb with a colander. Immediately

---

² Who's Bob?

7

the room is darker, but the light from inside is shining out through the holes in the colander and onto the ceiling, the walls, the books, and everything in the library. There are now little white dots everywhere.

Your friend comes in and sits on the couch with you.

As your eyes get adjusted to the new level of darkness, you notice that the colander in front of you isn't ordinary.

An ordinary colander has maybe 250 holes. This one has thousands. Instead of great big round circles of light everywhere, there are bright tiny diamonds on everything. Like the stars in the sky. It is very pretty.

Next, you notice that the light coming through the holes isn't just white. There are jewels and colored glass in the holes. The diamonds on the ceiling, the walls, books, and everything in the library are red, and green, and blue, and yellow, orange, purple, and every other color.
Thousands of colors shining through thousands of holes.

Then your friend says, "Here comes the best part."

The bright tiny diamonds on the ceiling, the walls, books, you, and everything in the library aren't just diamonds. Some are squares. Some are triangles. There's a "Z," a "4," a horse, a dash, a bicycle, a hammer, and every other shape and size. Thousands of holes in thousands of colors in thousands of shapes in all directions. It's a lot to take in.

You notice one more thing.

The colander rises a little off the table and becomes a whole sphere, about the size of a basketball; with the light bulb still inside it. The light bulb is shining out through twice as many holes now, with twice as many colors, and twice as many shapes and sizes.

Imagine it! A sphere floating in the middle of the room shining shapes on the table, on the ceiling, on the walls, the books, every corner, you, and everything else in the room everywhere in every color. It's magical!

Hold onto that. It is very important.
That is what we are. That's us. That is what we are.

The light bulb inside the sphere is life.
Each one of us is one of the tiny holes. We are a kind of lens.
We take the light of life and let it pass *through* us.
On the way through, we shape the light, color the light, change its intensity, direction… We form the light.

Our "personality" is the shape, color, direction, intensity… of the light of life we let pass through us, out to others, and out into the world.

We are expressions of the light of life. We express life.[3]

Now how much would you pay?! But wait! There's more!

Both or Nothing

There's a very important idea here. Let me show you.
Get up off the couch and get up close to the sphere.
Look closely into any hole.
The hole is open. The light is shining through it.
You can see the bulb inside, shining.

---

[3] It has a *lot* of other names: Atman, Cartesian Ego, The Christ, Emptiness, Father, The Field of all Possibilities, First Source, God, Goddess, God-in-us, The Ground of Substance and Being, Higher Power, It, Lord, Mind, Mother, Nature, The One, Soul, Spirit, Truth …

If you take away the bulb, you get darkness.
If you plug up the hole, you get darkness.
Either way you get darkness.

We need *both* the light *and* the hole.
One without the other is nothing.
We need the light; but the light needs us too.
That's the idea. Together, and *only* together, life is expressed.

Try #1 Summary

What we are:

We are an expression of life.
Each and every one of us is a unique and necessary expression of life.
We express life.

There are six other tries on my part to define what we are, back in Chapter 28. I suggest you leave them be and just go with this first definition.

If you are reading this for the first time, I very much recommend you do not just continue to the 2nd chapter. Let your head cool down a while first. Maybe even read chapter 1 again.

That, at least, is what I would do.
Thank you.

2. What God Is

Introduction

> If you want to make an apple pie from scratch, you must first create the universe.
> -Carl Sagan

"God" is an emotion-packed concept for everyone. Everyone has *feelings* about God. Lots of people hate God, fear God; God makes people *uncomfortable*. I tread on this ground with care, but I know I am going to offend to some extent everybody who reads this. So it goes. I yam what I yam.

When I was a boy, I was driving home with my father from the stationery store where he had just bought me my very first dictionary.

He told me a story about a dictionary he had when *he* was a boy.

If you looked up "camel," it said, "See 'dromedary.'"
If you looked up "dromedary," it said, "See 'camel.'"

Defining God is like that.
Defining God is difficult, maybe even impossible.
Defining God is the goal of human endeavor. Go figure! :-)

Let's try to define God

11

To define something, take different words that we already know and use them to describe the new word. For example: "Electrical current is the flow of electrons in a wire."

Defining "current" requires an understanding of three other words: *wire*, *electrons*, and *flow*. If we understand these three words, then we understand and have defined a new word: "current."

So, to define "God" we take other words that are not God and…Oops! That's the problem. Every word in every language is a name for some part of God. There are no words that are not God-words.

The fact that human reason can even grasp at the question, "What is God?" demonstrates human divinity.

There are those that sincerely, even fiercely believe that one cannot know God. To them, God is un-knowable. Some of the deepest thinkers I know about have this belief. I respect but do not share it. To me, to decide that a problem is un-solvable closes the door on its solution.

And look at the trend! Even the *tiniest* piece of God-knowledge makes the walls of the mind expand. Close-minded becomes small-minded. Small-minded becomes open-minded. Open-minded becomes enlightened! Each time we learn a little more about God our box gets bigger to fit the new larger concept. The effort to define God is worth doing. I say go for it.

I am not saying this is the only way to see God and all other ways are wrong. That would be close-minded. Every sincere image of God is worthy of honor, scrutiny, study, even worship. I will have a lot to say about multiple views of God a little later, but not now. This is *What God Is*. This is a better way to see God. It might be helpful to you. It has certainly been helpful to me.

I must also apologize in advance to another group of people reading this whom I know will be offended, and I'm sorry. There's no one word for them as a group, but they are people who have ended their search for God with a person. A lot of people have done that. I was one of them too, once. But I had to leave that camp, encouraged strongly by my person's own words: "I am the way and the truth and the life. No one comes to the Father except through me."

He was right, by the way; absolutely right. I danced with him for many years until I grew itchy. I had to find God and put God into my own words, not his. He was necessary for me to find God, but not sufficient.

I am, again, not saying other points of view are wrong. That would be like saying one kind of wine is right and all other kinds are wrong. Nothing of the sort.

What God is Not

HOME REMODELING METAPHOR WARNING

I'm going to re-model the kitchen. The old kitchen must be re-moved first. To make room for the better idea of God, we must first remove the old idea.
Please don your hardhats. Demolition will begin now.

The old image of God is this: *God-like-us*.
Say good-bye to that old idea.

God is not like us. God does not possess any human traits. God does not get angry, pleased, loving, merciful, or have any other emotions. God is not interested in us *or* our salvation.
God does not have hands, eyes, a face, or any other body parts.
God does not laugh. God does not smile.
God does not see, hear, or speak.

God does not get happy. We cannot make God happy.
We cannot please God. We cannot displease God.
God is not our father. God is not our mother.
God is not a he. God is not a she.
God does not punish. God does not reward.
God acts in our universe almost not at all.
In short, The Lord is not a lord.

The qualities of actions, emotions, parts, etc. are *human* qualities and while they are perfectly normal in a human being, they are not God qualities. They are human qualities and God is not human. God is way above and *way* beyond anything human. You see now why I call this a "demolition."

More than not being human, God is not anything in existence. Yet God is everything in existence.
Hang on to that. We'll come back in a moment.

The tendency to see and picture God as human has been a totally useful tool for forever. I honor it. It makes perfect sense. "God-like-us" images help people understand their place in existence. The first two words of the prayer Jesus taught those who asked him how to pray were, "Our Father."

But the time has come to get beyond that. Jesus spoke to a humanity 80 generations ago. Mohammad, over 50. We have made a lot of progress since then. We're smarter now. And the scientific understanding of what we are is exploding, especially in understanding the mechanics of brains and thinking.

As we learn more and more about what a human being is, God-in-us seems to become smaller and smaller, eventually to disappear.

This must not happen.
God is not small.
God-in-us is the opposite of small and cannot disappear.

14

Toss out any idea of God as human.
Say good-bye to the old image.
We need a bigger God.

It Gets Worse

When we quote from the Bible about people being "made in the image and likeness of God," that does not mean God is like us. God is *not* like us! Sorry.

God is not love. Not exactly, anyway. Hear me out.
There is a huge problem with *God is love*:
> the world is full of crap.
> And I mean *full*.

Is God sometimes loving and sometimes not?
Is crap a form of love?
Does God love only some people?
Only sometimes?
In only some places?
If God is love, what about slavery, poverty, cancer, sexual abuse, mental illness, sexual abuse of the mentally ill, and sixty other problems I'm sure we can name? *What about it*?!
If God is love, why do people suffer?! Why do people *die*?!

Rather than make up some rationale to explain how God can be love in a world full of crap, I'm calling for a very slight re-tooling of the idea.
More on this too in a later chapter. For now, God is not love.

Demolition done. Are you OK?

I understand that this is a lot to throw away; a tradition of God-images thousands of years old, but the whole idea of God needs to be brought into the 21st century.

Right now.

What God Is

It is by The One that all beings are beings. -Plotinus

There is nothing in all the universe that one can point to and say "That is God, there," yet every word in every language is a word for some aspect of God. Every sunrise, every chord of music, every baby, every flower, every sparkling drop of water, every smile, every laugh, every joy: God.

Everything that exists is in God and of God.

So, if everything is in God and of God, what is God itself? What is outside of everything that exists? Why, existence itself.

God is existence.
God is *is*.
God is "*is*-ness."
God is what makes "is" possible.
God is what makes be *be*.
God is the *act* of being, the *fact* of being.
Not "supreme being;" being*ness*.
People have been debating the question, "Does God exist?" for tens of centuries.
The answer is *both* "No," *and* "Yes."[4]

God is not *in* existence. God does not exist. So, "No."
God is *existence*. Does existence exist? Yes. So, "Yes."

God is existence. Get your head around it, folks. You can do it.

It is interesting to note that in the Exodus bible book when Moses asked God what God's name was, God answered, "I Am."

---

[4] Lots of questions have more than one answer. This is just another one of them.

16

Now Here's the Cool Thing

Do we exist? *Of course* we do!
Since we do, we are like God. Got it?
We are like God! You are like God! You are God-like!

God is not like us. We are like God!

Have you heard of the field of gravity?
A magnetic field? An electric field, perhaps?
God is the field of existence.

And That's Enough

Being beingness is enough to make God God.
Beingness is a big deal, a monster deal.

To convert something into something else? Easy. Minor.

The leap from *nothing* into *something*? Major. *Uber* major.
Bigger than that.

But Not All

To understand God as existence may not fully encompass all
of God, but it's enough for now. "What's outside of existence?"
can wait until existence is more fully understood, someday.
Once we've fully explored the closet we're sitting in now, we
can then leave it to explore the bedroom the closet is in.

What Does God Look Like?

Interesting thing about human beings:
Everyone knows what God looks like.
To them.

It is vital to have an image of God *within*, and we all do.

God-within is what separates us from machines, and we all have it, God-within.

People are fiercely loyal to their image of God, and everyone has one, even people whose image is *no-image*.

Our image is usually the one we were given and took in as children. People get together with others who have similar God-images and call themselves group-names like Christians, Muslims, Atheists, Jews, Unitarians, Buddhists, Agnostics…
It's very individual, and very social, both at the same time.

But be careful.
Loyalty to an image is self-defeating. Don't limit yourself.
An image limits God, and God is limit-less.
Get yourself a bigger image of God.
How about this one: God is existence.

The Problem with Prayer

While we are at the task of defining a better image of God, prayer needs work too.

Prayer is a great thing. Prayer is how people open themselves up, commune with the divine; connect to the divine in them.

The problem is this: the usual way to pray is a mistake and almost always a total waste. The usual way to pray is for us "on earth" to ask for something from God "in heaven."

Or we might send out thank-you's to God, again, up in heaven. Up there. Not here.

The problem is the imagined separation between us and God that doesn't exist. We think God is apart from us, up there in heaven, and we're down here on Earth. That is *so* not it!

God is existence.

We are woven into God and God is woven into us.
All is you and me and every piece of you and every piece of me. There is no separation. We cannot *not* be in God.

The problem with prayer goes even deeper though. When we pray for something, we are asking God to act on our behalf:
> Give us
> Forgive us
> Lead us
> Lead us not

If God were like a superhuman he could do all that stuff.
But he's *not* like a superhuman. He's not even a *he*.

God does not act.
We act. Or we don't.

When we ask God to hear our prayers, we are asking God to listen.
God does not listen.
We listen. Or we don't.

When we thank God for benefits received, God does not hear our gratitude. God does not hear. God does not give.
We hear. We give. Or not.

By praying to God up in heaven we are shooting our prayers in the wrong direction. God is not up there. Haven't you ever wondered why your prayers are never answered?

To reach God, pray *inwards*, *towards* that shining light of life.
Tell yourself that you are loving and loved. Feel love.
Tell yourself that you have the resources. Feel abundant.
Tell yourself that you can do what needs to be done. Feel capable.
Tell yourself "Thank you." Feel gratitude.
God is closer to us than we are to ourselves.
Look within. Thou art the buddha, literally, "one who's awake."

I saw a book in a store once. Its title was *Paths to God*. I am sure the author of this book meant no harm, but to proclaim "there is a path to God" is to proclaim there is a distance to God. There ain't.

There is no distance between That and thou.
There is no distance between Thee and me.
There is no path to God but to *be*.
We *are*. We are in God. That's it. Welcome home.

> Speak to him thou for He hears
> And Spirit with Spirit can meet.
> Closer is He than breathing,
> And nearer than hands and feet.[5]

A Summary

In this little chapter I have tried to un-seat a deeply-felt religious belief held by a large part of humanity for thousands of years. Good luck with that one, eh? :-)

Nevertheless, here it is and it's where I stand. It makes sense; to me, anyway. If it doesn't make sense to you, I apologize for my lack of clarity.

God can be understood.

Our understanding of God, whatever it may be, must *make sense*, not just rely on faith or fear or tradition.

Faith is good. Faith is great.
Faith with understanding is far, far greater.
Fear has no part at all in *any* understanding of God. At least, it shouldn't have. Can't say that it doesn't have. Lots of religions are based at least in part on fear.

---

[5] Tennyson.

20

I do not feel obliged to believe that the same God who has endowed us with sense, reason, and intellect has intended us to forgo their use. -Galileo Galilei (1564-1642)

Here in a few short sentences is what God is.

- God is not an entity.
- God is existence, being-ness; that which makes be *be*.
- God is not like us. We are like God.
- There is more to God, but being-ness is enough for now.
- Be careful not to hold onto your God-image too tightly.
- GodInUsInGod.
- God is closer to us, and we are closer to God, than the air we breathe. We could not be closer.

Welcome home.

3. What It's All About

God walks into a bar. The bartender says, "What'll it be?" Seven days later…

This one is about meaning. You know: What's it all for? If there isn't some sort of reason for all of this existence, then it's an enormous waste of space and time.

Here's one answer.

First, you gots to remember somethin' I be tryin' to tell ya. They ain't no separation between "the world" and "us." I done said this already.

It sure *seems* like there is a distance between "me" and "what's out there." We look through our eyes and see things we want that are beyond our reach. We can't have them. They must be separate from us. It also seems like there is a distance between "you" and "me."

But that separation is a squiggly illusion. And that's not necessarily a bad thing. It's an illusion we want and often need. Life may have hurt us. Life may be currently hurting us. Life seems to hurt everybody. We may very much *need* to feel separated and protected from what's out there.

But a necessary illusion is still a lie; like being polite to people we don't like. It's necessary, but it's bogus.

Life is a continuous stream, a flow of time and space where everything is eventually connected to everything else. Our computing machine brains need to have separations and categories to deal with all the facets of life. Our brains need to see life as a series of blocks: blocks of time, blocks of objects, blocks of tasks, blocks of words…

We bust existence into pieces, name the pieces, categorize them, file them, deal with them…
As a continuous stream, life is too much to deal with, too much to take in. But taken in chunks, life is computable.

Or is it? Why do we need to think, anyway?
Can't we just … know … now … and get on to something else?

A bowl of soup and a sandwich walk into a bar.
The bartender says, "We don't serve lunch here."

We are connected to God and God is connected to us.
We are wired in to life in a bajillion ways;
and life is thoroughly part of us. We're home, here.

We are in God. God is in us. It's easy to say, difficult to comprehend. Both are true, yet how can syrup be in a jar, that is in a jar made of syrup? Sounds crazy.

Here's an example of how to un-tie this knot: SpongeBob SquarePants. Bob is a sponge *in the ocean*. He is surrounded by ocean in every direction, just as we are surrounded by God. But! Or And! Bob is a *sponge*, which means the ocean is *in Bob*. Bob is *filled* with ocean, as we are filled with God.

Let it be. Let it flow. Be quiet for just a moment and feel the unity, a unity we are all a part of.

Once we see that we are *in* life and life is in *us, what it's all about* is a whole lot easier to grasp.

Life is cool, life is unbiased. Life doesn't care what life is all about. Life just *is* and that's that.

We, however, need an answer.

23

If you want to know what life is all about,
open your mouth and say it,
and that's your answer.

Lots of people have already done this.

"Life is about service to others," said Albert Einstein, Earl Nightingale, Jesus of Nazareth, Dolly Parton, Bill W, and lots of other people.

"Life is about learning," say others. Good teachers think that.

"Life is about loving," say lots of songwriters.
I kinda like that one.

"Life is about loss and fear and addiction and hunger and cold and danger and death and screwing them before they screw you, and then you *die*," say lots of people.
Your choice if you want to believe that or not.

And that's the answer in two words.
What's life about? *Your choice.*

What do you *choose* life to be about? Go ahead and choose.
And then say it out loud.

The meaning of life is the meaning we give it.
The purpose of life is to love and live in it.

> A priest, a rabbi, and a minister walk into a bar.
> The bartender says, "What is this, a joke?"

4. Part 2. So, What?

After the theory comes the practice.

> In theory, there is no difference between theory and practice.
> In practice, there is.
> -Yogi Berra

5. A Psalm of Life

A Psalm of Life
by Henry Wadsworth Longfellow
What the Heart of a Young Man Said to a Psalmist

Henry Wadsworth Longfellow was a rock star in his time. Bigger than that. His birthday was a national holiday, even while he was still alive. He wrote *A Psalm of Life* in 1838. I have updated the wording in a few places.

Tell me not in mournful numbers,
"Life is but an empty dream!"
For the soul is dead that slumbers,
And things are *so* not what they seem.

Life is real! Life is earnest!
And the grave is not its goal;
"Dust thou art and dust returnest,"
Was not spoken by the soul.

Not for joy and not for sorrow
Is our destined end and way;
But to *act*, that each to-morrow
Finds us further than to-day.

Art is long and time is fleeting
And though our hearts be stout and brave,
Still, like muffled drums they're beating
Funeral marches to the grave.

In the world's broad fields of battle,
In the locker rooms of life,

Be not dumb and driven cattle!
Be a hero in the strife!

Trust no Future, howe'er pleasant.
Let the Past be passed and gone.
Act – act *now* in the living Present.
Hearts uplifted, full of song.

Lives of noble ones remind us
We can make our lives sublime,
And, departing, leave behind us
Footprints on the sands of time;

Footprints, that perhaps another,
Stumbling through life's troubled plain,
Seeing that they have a brother,
Will take heart and try again.

Let us, then, be up and doing!
With a heart for any fate;
Still achieving, still pursuing,
Learn and labor, to be great!

6. The Allness of God

The "allness" of God is a tough one to hang on to because there's nothing like it anywhere. Let's start.

Every thing in the world has edges. A pencil on a table has edges. There's the pencil, there's the table, there's the place where they touch: all edges.

A carton of milk in the refrigerator has edges.
A book, our hands, our eyes: edges.
Time has edges too; a day, a season, a year.

Every thing has edges.

God is not a thing. God doesn't have edges. When we go to look for God, we don't see God because: no edges. Our eyes are looking for edges and there aren't any anywhere to see.

When we see a chair in the kitchen, the chair is in one place; and not anywhere else. This is simple, so far. If God were a thing, we would see God in one place, there, and not anyplace else. But God is here and there and *everywhere* else. God just doesn't have edges. Tough to see, without edges.

But we *can* see God if we look with the right eyes. We can see God all the time.

We see separate things: tree, sidewalk, grass, sky, face, hand... We see them and name them because that's what our brains need to do to comprehend stuff. We need to see everything as *pieces*. Pieces have edges. We understand the pieces, we put the pieces together, and we understand the whole.

But "piecing" is something we invented. We made it up! A tree is a thing. But a tree is also the soil and the sky. The tree and the soil and the sky are all one, if we look at it that way. And we can. The edges around the tree got bigger just now.

When we name a thing, we "embox" it. We separate it from other things it connects to. It's necessary maybe to understand it; but it's a separation we made up ourselves. We break existence into pieces to think about it, and it works; but not here where we're working with all of God, all of existence.

The ancient Hebrews refused to write out the name of God because they did not want to squeeze God into a box. Some people refuse to "name" God even today.

Seeing God is like seeing darkness at night. We usually don't see darkness, but with the right eyes we'll go "*D'oh*! Darkness! There it is! Of course!" Everywhere.

God is like that. Everywhere. No edges. All.
Every thing has edges. Everything does not.

God is is. This is a new kind of theism. Well, not *totally* new. St. John of the Cross[6] wrote, "God is not a being, God *is* being."

Go practice.
Look through your eyes. You're seeing God.
Listen through your ears. You're hearing God.
Smell through your smeller. You're smelling God.
You know what I mean! Everything that is is an aspect of God.

---

[6] (1542-1592)

7. God is Love?

Another hard one. I don't know if there *are* any easy ones.

The concept, "God is love," is the very core of Christian and Muslim theology. *Is* God love?

That depends; on us.

Are we loving? Do we see love? Do we feel love? Do we accept love? Then God is love. To us.

Are we nervous? Jumpy? Skittish? Anxious?
Then by all means God is not love. Again, to us.

It is a good thing to think that God is love. Whatever image of God we hold in our heart is going to show up in our life everywhere. Hold the sun. That's why people are endlessly proclaiming "the love of God," or "The Lord be with you." If we faith it, it becomes so; goodness made real, because of faith.

But it's up to us! It's a choice. How loving or how devilish is life, really? We decide what to love and what to fear. We decide what is good and what is evil. We decide how dangerous the world is, or how loving.

Us. Not God. And *that's* the hard part.
God is existence; *astonishingly* neutral.
God just is. The only verb God verbs is "be."
The rest, is up, to us.

Many have seen the wonderful benefits that come from the faith that God is in charge, that God is love, that our Father in Heaven loves us, protects us, and cares for us.
Believing is seeing.

Many others have felt the crushing burdens of a life filled with doubt and fear. Addiction. Chronic pain. Depression.

But it's us, *our* decisions, not God making things happen.
We lift ourselves up. We hold ourselves down.
Sometimes both at the same time.
By all means lift yourself up!
But God *is*, and that's it. The rest is up to us.

Except, except, except for one thing: *life*.[7]
Let me explain.

There's a science fact that has a fancy name: *The Second Law of Thermodynamics*. Water always flows downhill. Steel always rusts. Drop a brick and it always falls. Wood always burns to ash. Eggs cook to an omelet.

Ash never burns to wood.
Omelets never become eggs.
Water never runs uphill.
It never goes backwards.

Almost never.

The word "law" doesn't mean somebody enacted something and has police out there to enforce it. Rather, a "law" in science means, "We've seen this happen over and over and over again. It's predictable. It's reliable. It's dependable. It's a law."

----

[7] I didn't say one *little* thing. :-)

There is another law that supersedes the Second Law. It is predictable, reliable, and dependable too. I don't know if *it* has a fancy name, but it goes like this: Nature Wants Better.

Nature Wants Better

Big Bang. Everything started out so freaking hot there weren't even particles,
Then it cooled a bit and we got atoms.
Then, stars.
Then elements.
Then planets.
Then life,
Then complex life,
Then us.

There's a progression here, a path, a direction: *Improvement*. There are mechanisms in place that enforce this. Nature Wants Better. Nature goes for better. Not everything flows downhill. Life swims upstream.

Each generation is slightly smarter than the previous one. Problems pop up and get solved. We long for, and work towards, a better life. We each know what Better looks like (to us) and we are all striving for Better.

One can say that Nature Wants Better is God's love woven into the very marrow of existence. When we want better, and we want better all the time, we reflect this law of nature.[8] It's *within* us. In a way, we *can* say there is a will of God: to be better. We can say that God *wants* something: better. Sure seems that way. Better is the goal. Better is the task. Better is our job to do.

---

[8] Because people are so *emotional* about the word "God," I sometimes use other words instead of "God," like "Nature," "Existence," "Life," "the Universe," "Everything," "42," "Douglas Adams,"…

But what about evil? What about cancer, child abuse, mental illness, human trafficking, disease, poverty, hunger, racism, …

We work at it. We fix it. Fixing problems is good. We don't find God by doing things right. We find God by doing things wrong *and fixing them.* God is found in the fix. Evil is necessary. Evil has a purpose. Evil gives us a reason to be better, a mission, a goal, a call to duty, something to do. Pain pushes. Therefore, is evil *evil*?

As always, we get to choose.

Is it a problem, or is it a challenge?
Do we *have* to do it, or do we *get* to do it?
Is it a limit, or is it a goal?
Is it an obstacle, or is it an opportunity?
A mistake, or something to learn from?
A loss, or a gain in some other direction?

Our choice. Let love guide.

If there is ever going to be love in the world, *and there damn well* better *be love in the world*, we must choose the loving choice. We must make the love. It's too bad that "to make love" in American English means "to have sex," because there is so much more to making love than making love.

It is very comforting to think that the core of existence is loving, has our best interests at heart, is nurturing, is sustaining, mothering, blah blah blah.

"God is love" is *almost* right. Add two more words to it, and we are there.
God is love *through us*.
If that's what we decide.
If you want God to be love, be loving. Decide to love.

8. What about Thinking?

I think, therefore I am. *I think*. –Moody Blues

Take a car apart to see how it works and you've broken it. Same with any toy, a TV, a person… We are *one*. We only work as *one*. There may be pieces, but the pieces need to be strung together into *one* in order to work.

So be careful when you read me writing, "we are composed of three parts." We are *one*. The three "parts," and the parts those parts are composed of, are *not us*. They are our parts.

We are composed of three parts: Mind, Body, and Spirit.
I wrote them in that order because it corresponds exactly with the "three persons in one God" belief I used to hold.
Father, Son, Holy Spirit: Mind, Body, Spirit.

Mind is seeing, hearing, remembering, reasoning, thinking…
Body is brain, nerves, heart, lungs, legs, arms, hair, skin…
Spirit is your connection to all that is.

Like I said: We are one. Take away any part and we stop.

Let us think about thinking. Mind. Plato thought the mind was a tree and thoughts were birds flying around amongst the branches. In my lifetime, mind science has become a science.

We are not our mind. We are not *in* our mind. Go look. We are mind, through body, to spirit, and back. One. If you need to think of yourself as one thing, think "I am a connection to

God." Didn't I say this already once? No. Well I will, later. What I said was "You express God." Same thing.

The mind, thinking, has many levels, as science is learning. I want to focus on the lowest level, the limbic system, the so-called "lizard brain" or "gut level."

There are two emotions here that drive the whole rest of our lives. They are root concepts. They come with the package, like thumbs or earlobes. If you want a simple way to control your life, here's where you work. Note I said "simple," not easy.

Love. Fear. Love and Fear. Love or Fear. Love. Fear.

We love because we love.
For the same reason we breathe, we need to love to live.
We fear because we do. It too is a part of you.

What we think is *important*. Reality is what we accept as real, and "what we accept as real" is what we *think* is real.

This is the most empowering idea ever invented and I wish it had been me that invented it.[9]
We can change our reality by changing our thinking.
In fact, it is the only way to change our reality.
Saying it in nine words does not mean it is easy to do,
but it is do-*able*.
We can change our reality by changing our thinking.

How?

Love and Fear. Love or Fear.

This bottom level determines the structure of our lives. What we love and what we fear defines us. We determine our reality

[9] I think it was William James (1842-1910).

by what we love and what we fear. You want to change you? Change the balance between love and fear.
You want to *improve* you? Love more, fear less.

I do not know anything about you; your life, your childhood, your dreams, your desires, your goals, your mama drama or anything else about you except this: your life will improve when you love more and fear less.

So simple to say! So difficult to do!

From years of trying, I have the following method.
You are welcome to it.

The love will take care of itself. Don't worry about the love.
Reduce your fear.

Whittle away at it. Spend your time reducing your fear.
Fear less.

The way, the *only* way to do that is to *face* your fear. Act. Do the thing you are afraid to do. Do things that you are scared to do. Nothing else works. Do the thing you are afraid to do.

If you find something you're afraid of, you've just found something to do.

Simple. Not easy. Sorry. I'm just the messenger. Act.
Actions will guide your thoughts much better than your thoughts will guide your actions. Act as if.

Once you do the thing you fear, the fear goes away. *Poof*!
A little less fear is a little more love.

9. What about Jesus?

Jesus was the most famous person who ever lived.
For good reason.
But…
Jesus would be horrified to see what we've done with Him.
We've missed His point. I don't think He ever intended to be
glorified into God-Man. His followers called him "Teacher."
He never said "Worship me." He said "Follow me."

It makes sense, though. We are humans. We *need* exaltedness.
We need to look upwards and see a human face smiling down
on us. I'm not sure why, but look at the evidence. We have
Popes and Presidents and Celebrities and Heroes and Royals
and Movie Stars and Gold Medal Olympic Champions and this
is not a bad thing at all! People need people to look up to! We
even plaster a human face on God!

But please, not Jesus' face! Exalting Him hides His message!
We need to look eye-to-eye at the man from Galilee, not up.
Equal beings.

Consider the fact that Jesus was an ordinary man, as divine as
you or I. What a wonder is the glory of God that an ordinary
man could work miracles!

What an even greater wonder and glory is the fact that we can
work miracles too with the right understanding of God. That is
what He was trying to teach us. That was His point.

Jesus referred to Himself as "the way." His earliest followers
referred to themselves as "the people of The Way." They understood what He was trying to say: this is the way to God. Not
to Jesus; to God.

Somewhere along the way Jesus got changed from "the way" to "the destination." Ooops!

This is bad on so many levels, but the worst one is this: exalting Jesus to God-level gives us an excuse to not do the things He tried to show us how to do. Deify Jesus and we can say, "Jesus stilled the water and healed the sick and multiplied the bread and rose from the dead because He was God, and since I am not God, I cannot do those things."

But thou *art* God, the highest form of God's expression. We are divine and nothing less. Putting Jesus above us leads to endless (and pointless) fighting about Jesus the God-Man. Born of a virgin? Divine? Human? Both? Resurrected? Twin brother?

And with all that distraction, the most important question goes un-asked: How do I get His understanding of God, his "kingdom of heaven"?

It's all About Power

Jesus tried to show us the ways to God. He had a very good idea what He was talking about. Making Him *into* God and then building a church around Him means someone else has control over our access to God, not us. But only if we let them.

I am no history scholar, I do not claim to be, but I know a power play when I see one. Somewhere in the early Christian church's history the leaders of the church had to decide whether they were going to take the paths that lead to God, or the path that leads to power, based on everyone's desire to find God.

The men of the church (and they were all men) had to decide whether to be ser*vants* or ser*vers*. "Do we give it away or do we sell it?"

They took the second path: "We have the way to God and if you follow our rules, we will let you see it."
And for the most part, people just accept this. *Grrrr*.

If somebody's idea of Jesus is standing between you and God, take a step to the side and look around it. *God* is the goal, not Jesus.

Though I do not know as much about Mohammed as I have learned about Jesus, I see the signs of man-worship in Islam as well. Death threats to an artist who draws a picture of The Prophet? Death threats to an author who writes a story about The Prophet? What is being worshipped here, The God, or God's Messenger?

God cannot be harmed by anything. God neither needs nor takes vengeance. God does not need to be defended.
But an image of God? Ah…another story.
Looks like man-worship to me. Again.

> God is a comedian playing to an audience too afraid to laugh.
> -Voltaire (1694-1778)

To Those Who Go to Services

There are many good reasons to attend worship: the social nature, the chance to join with others in charitable works, the music, teach the kids to be good, the chance to be a part of something bigger than yourself.

And the best reason of all: to worship; alongside others who worship with you.

It is time to turn outwards and see God in everything, all around. Ask your house of worship if they can show you how to do that. Maybe it already does.

We are divine. More divine than we think we are. Ask your house of worship if they can show you that. Maybe it can.

We are one with God. We are like God. God shines through us. Does your house of worship teach you these things? If it does, keep attending. If it does not, go find one that does.
Or start one of your own. Learn your divinity.

To Those Who Don't Go to Services

There are many good reasons to not belong to a house of worship. It's boring. It doesn't make any sense. The music stinks. It's full of hypocrites who smile to your face and stab you in the back. Everybody fights with everybody else. It's not the truth. And the biggest reason of all: it's a waste of time.

Do you see God anywhere? Can you expand on that?
Do you know all parts of you are divine?
Do you see divinity in *any* parts of you?
Do you feel the presence of God *any*where? Everywhere?[10]

If you do not, maybe it's time to get some help.
Find a place to worship? Or start one of your own?
Learn your divinity.

---

[10] Another word for feeling the presence of God everywhere is "immanence."

10. What's Your POV?

Nature gave most of us two eyes.
Cover one eye. Look around.
You can still see.
But everything looks the same distance away.
Everything looks flat, the same distance away.
There's no depth.

Open your eye.

With two eyes, each eye sees the same thing from a slightly different angle. With the little differences between what the two eyes see, our brain calculates how near and far things are. We see depth. The brain is amazing like that. Try that again.

It takes two eyes to see things in three dimensions.
Seeing God is like that. It takes different points of view.

When Jesus was just newly gone, His disciples split up in all directions. There was one sect, the Ebionites, that believed you had to follow the Law of Moses to find God.

There was another sect, the Marcionites, that believed the Law of Moses was superseded and must *not* be followed in order to find God.

There was a third sect, the Gnostics, who believed that the God described by Jesus was so different from the God of the Hebrew Scriptures, there simply must be two Gods.

There were even stranger sects as well. Look up Docetism.[11]

---

[11] http://en.wikipedia.org/wiki/Docetism

It turns out that what we now call "orthodox" Christianity borrowed from all these sects. There was value in each point of view (POV).

That's my point. There is value in every point of view.
Even differing ones.
More than that. We cannot see God to any depth with only our own one point of view.

And the cool thing here is this: give people freedom of religion and churches of all kinds pop up all over the place. POV city!

It takes a tough person to be open to the possibility that something they strongly disagree with might be at least partly right. Not either/or; both/and.

God is so multi-faceted, no one person can see God in all detail. It takes a lot of different opinions to get a decent view of what God is all about. That's why Jesus said to love our *enemies*.[12] Their point of view is valuable; *very* valuable simply because it is so different from ours. *Every* point of view is valuable.

In other words, *your* point of view is valuable. You matter. You are the only one who can be you, who can see what it is *you* see.

I think most people are not seeing God. I see their faces. "The mass of men lead lives of quiet desperation." If you don't see God, you don't see your *self*, you don't see your *center*, you don't see your *core*. Most people I'm afraid, do not.

There's a way out of that. Let's walk it together.

_____

[12] Matthew 5:44, Luke 6:27.

41

Start with you are valuable, your point of view is valuable.

The next time you hear about a movement to "unify" the churches, or hear the phrase "the one true church," shake your head knowingly, smile, and walk quietly past. It takes more than one point of view to see God in all of God's fullness. They just don't understand that yet.

11. What's Up?

Fourteen Words to Higher

Don't glorify God for God's sake. God doesn't need it.
Glorify ourselves. We *do* need it.
And anyway, glorifying us glorifies God, so it's a win-win.

I want to teach you, tell you, show you, *convince* you that you
are glorious. I can't do that without your help of course.

Theory is one thing. But if you want the theory to become real,
you have to *practice* it, *do* it. Faith *and* works. Understanding
and service. We have a saying in MA:
> Sobriety doesn't come to those who want it.
> Sobriety doesn't come to those who need it.
> Sobriety comes to those who *work* it.

Here are seven helpful two-word phrases to print out and pin
up on your refrigerator. Slowly, slowly, slowly they will work
their way into our self-images and we will heal.

Whadda ya got to lose? Fourteen words. *It couldn't hoit.*
First, the phrases, in alphabetical order.

> Be Grateful
> Equal Beings
> Fear Teaches
> I'm Responsible
> Love Yourself
> No Resistance
> See Love

Now the details.

Be Grateful

If you're grateful, you can't help but be happy.
Foster an attitude of gratitude.

This is very easy some of the time,
and *very hard* some of the time.
It's the very hard times I want to talk about here.

We do not know what's going to happen next. We do not *ever* know what's going to happen next. We like to think that we do, but we don't. Ever. All we know is, life is change.

A very hard time is when it's easy to see that bad times are coming. Or in the bad times, it looks like something even worse is coming.

But that's still just a prediction, a projection, a forecast. *Anything* can happen. And by expecting hard times, we are already experiencing them.

Miracles can happen at any time with absolutely no warning. Be grateful.

Make it easier on yourself. When you see bad times a-comin', say "Good. There's a deep lesson to be learned here. I will, and I'll wind up better for it." Be grateful.

For example: my mother's death. While she was dying, in the midst of the horror and the emptiness, I was able to at least allow for the possibility that good things would come from it. "Something good will come from this."
Turns out, in an unexpected way, I grew closer to my sister.
I am grateful.

44

Example #2. The worst thing that ever happened to me (so far) was the end of my first marriage. I was a zombie for years. But it taught me enormous lessons about myself. In a roundabout way it led to my being able to break my addiction to marijuana.[13] And it pointed me to my second wife. I would have never known my sons had I not gotten divorced. I couldn't be more grateful for my divorce, the worst tragedy of my life.
Be grateful.

I'm not saying the good times show up on demand. It took me years to recover from my divorce and I am still not fully recovered from my mother's death two decades later. There are bad times in my life I will never recover from. You too.

But be grateful. Bad times take you to places within you that you would *never* go to on your own. And there, you will learn lessons. Learn the lesson and the pain will lessen. Be grateful.

Our attitude determines our altitude. It's a powerful defense against the often-frequent times when shit falls from the sky. We'll find a way to sell it for fertilizer. Be grateful.

Equal Beings

This is another hard one. Come to think of it, they're *all* hard. Buck up. We can do this.

"Equal beings" is based on the fact that you and I are expressions of the same soul. We weren't just created equal, we are *currently* equal, even when we don't see it.

Equal beings is seeing that hot fox coming up the corridor, and knowing that you and they are on the same plane, in the same

---

[13] My name is Lionel and I am a marijuana addict. Clean and sober 39 years. And if you do not understand this footnote, be very, *very* grateful.

big room, passengers on the same bus. You have nothing to fear from them and they have nothing to fear from you.

Equal beings is seeing that big scary-ugly man coming towards you in the alleyway and knowing that you and he share the same fears, and laugh at the same jokes on *The Simpsons*. A big scary-ugly man would be very grateful to see someone look him in the eye without fear for a change.

Equal beings is seeing that blind man who sits near the top of the escalator at the Prudential Center T stop every freaking day and know that our struggle is just as hard as his is. Life is hard for everyone.

Equal beings is waiting for a job interview, or a hearing on a traffic ticket, or for that cop who just pulled you over; and knowing that you have more in common with the boss, the judge, the cop, than you know. We are all lumps in the same gravy.

Our money doesn't make us better.
Our poverty doesn't make us worse.
We are already divine. There's no more we need to do.
We are equal beings.

Fear Teaches

Wouldn't it be nice if we had some sort of Spirit Guide or something that would sit on our shoulder and tell us what to do whenever we needed guidance?

We do. We absolutely do! It is *so cool*!

We all have fear! And fear is a freaking *guide*!

Whatever your fear is telling you to do, do the opposite!
Whatever your fear is telling you *not* to do, do that!

Whenever I go to a restaurant, I look for things on the menu I have never had before. And I try them. This plan works for me almost always and because of it, I have had goat, rabbit, frog, snake, chicken tikka masala pizza, squid, buffalo, …

Following our fear in the opposite direction is a guide. Let it teach you. It works far more times than it fails. And oh, the places you'll go…

I'm Responsible

It's your life. You can live it and blame everyone around you, or you can stand up and take responsibility for it.

Mommy may have done cocaine when you were *in utero.*
Uncle Ernie may have touched you in places unspeakable.
Daddy may have come home drunk all the time, or not at all.
You may have been born with only a thumb on your left hand or somebody or something took it off.
You may be EMR, or have ADD, or ADHD, or AIDS.
You have perfectly good excuses for being the person you think you are. Everybody feels that way. Got it. Fine.
Now what? How long do you want to suffer?!

Accept you for you as you are. You give away your power when you make "them" responsible for the state of your life. It's *your* life, not theirs. If you give persons or circumstances the power to hurt you, you give them the power to limit you. They have no such power until you give it to them. Don't. "*I'm* responsible for me."

We are limit-less. All you have to do is understand that you are. Make yourself responsible for you and you get all your power back. We can go anywhere, do anything, be anybody.

I'm responsible. If you're willing to take the responsibility, you get the authority and the power.

Love Yourself

The hardest thing in the world is for you to love yourself.
Love yourself anyway.

Nobody knows you better than you do. You are a witness to all the stupid, shameful, terrible, bone-headed, ugly things you've ever done. Nobody knows how guilty you are. Nobody knows how much you deserve to be punished.
Love yourself anyway.

Nobody knows better than you do how un-loveable you are. Nobody knows how afraid you are, how sad you are, how angry you are, how sick you are, how lonely you are *oh*, so much of the time.
Love yourself anyway.

Nobody knows how hard it is for you to love anything. Things you love turn around and hurt you.
Love yourself anyway.

Love yourself for not being able to love yourself.

Stop waiting for somebody else to love you first.
You love you first.

Nobody and nothing is keeping score, in heaven, or on Earth. Only you, and you're always looking at the bad side of you. Give yourself a freaking break! Love yourself.

If you can't go all the way to *love*, find something you *like* about yourself and build up to love from there. You can do this.

The hardest thing in the world is for you to love yourself.

Love yourself anyway.

No Resistance

No Resistance is a weird one because it goes against logic. Logic dictates we fight the things that get in our way; but logic is a trickster. Whatever you resist persists. If we let the things in our way just be, with acceptance and love, they will transform. Dissolve evil with good, not anger, hatred, revenge…

Remember, it's *your* reality. Reality is what *you* accept as real. A roadblock, an impediment, a barrier, a problem, is a problem because you *see* it as a problem. If you can see it as an opportunity, it stops being a problem immediately. Psychologists call this a "re-frame." One man's ceiling is another man's floor.

Don't say "I *have* to …"
Say "I *get* to …"
It changes your whole point of view.

Seeing all problems as opportunities is a way of life and not easy to do at first. But you can start small. What's your most-recent setback? Was there a lesson there that maybe you missed? Is there anything about it you can turn to your advantage? Is there any hidden message in it?

When you put your fists up to fight, you block your vision.
Drop your fists.
Is there something there now that you didn't see before?

Look carefully. Accept with love. Be willing to have it so. Let it be. No resistance.

See Love

This one is going to take a Bible reference. Four, actually; all taken from the Contemporary English Version.[14]

- Listen, Israel! The Lord our God is the only true God! So, love the Lord your God with all your heart, soul, and strength. Memorize his laws. (Deu 6:4-6)

- Then one of them, which was a lawyer, asked him a question, tempting him, and saying, "Master, which is the great commandment in the law?" Jesus said unto him, "Thou shalt love the Lord thy God with all thy heart, and with all thy soul, and with all thy mind." (Matthew 22:34-37)

- One of the teachers of the Law of Moses came up while Jesus and the Sadducees were arguing. When he heard Jesus give a good answer, he asked him, "What is the most important commandment?" Jesus answered, "The most important one says: 'People of Israel, you have only one Lord and God. You must love him with all your heart, soul, mind, and strength.'" (Mark 12:28-30)

- An expert in the Law of Moses stood up and asked Jesus a question to see what he would say. "Teacher," he asked, "what must I do to have eternal life?" Jesus answered, "What is written in the Scriptures? How do you understand them?" The man replied, "The Scriptures say, 'Love the Lord your God with all your heart, soul, strength, and mind.' They also say, 'Love your neighbors as much as you love yourself.'" Jesus said, "You have given the right answer. If you do this, you will have eternal life." (Luke 10:25-28)

---

[14] Scripture quotations are from the Contemporary English Version, Copyright © 1991, 1992, 1995 by American Bible Society, Used by Permission. I get to say that.

See a pattern here? What does it mean to "love the Lord your God"? Does it mean tossing your emotions up into the sky towards a white-robed old man with a long white beard? Uh, no.

Look around you. *There* is the Lord your God. In every direction. Far away, near at hand, large, small, loving, fearful, green, purple...*Everything*[15] is an expression of "the Lord your God." Can't get away from it. We are in God.

Look with eyes of love. Touch with hands of love. Listen with ears of love. Help each other with lives of love.

A dude drives by at the wheel of a powder blue Mercedes-Benz CL560.
Do you say, "There's *another* thing I'm never going to have!"?
Do you say, "He must be kissing some righteous ass to get that car."?
Do you say, "Hmmm. What would it take to steal that?"

Or do you say, "Look at that breath-taking expression of beauty, creativity, and craftsmanship. Nice color, too." (OK, so that's a bit over the top. How about "*Whoa! Bodacious!*")

If your reality is going to be filled with love, you are going to have to do the filling; with every think you thinks.

See love. We cannot control the images, but we can control the meaning, our response. See love everywhere, and everywhere will be an expression of love.

This is easy to do.
Baby's faces. Spring mornings. Christmas lights on houses.
With these things it is easy to see love.

---

[15] ...and every thing...

This is hard to do.
Sometimes almost impossible, like when the bombs go off and your ears are ringing and pieces of legs and people are lying all around you. How do you see love here?

How *do* you see love here?!
By loving what you see!
Love the care-givers! Love the first responders! Love the injured! Love the hand that holds the tourniquet; that cradles the head; that pushes the stretcher towards the hospital. Love the hurt. Cover the hurt with love like you cover your waffles with syrup!

It was an inability (or a refusal) to *see love* that caused the bombs to be made and exploded in the first place. *Refuse* to continue the pattern. Stand firm in your understanding that We Control the Meaning. *Here*, *Right Here* is the Lord your God!

If you don't love what you see, love what you see.
Inject love into it. It needs it.

See love.

12. What's Good in All This *What.* Stuff?

What I am proposing with all this ranting is a redefinition of God. Well, maybe not a re-definition, more like a re-wording of God: some better synonyms for God.

Let's look at God in a new way.
And in the process, let's look at us in a new way too.

I am doing this for two reasons that I can think of.

One. Orthodox religion is collapsing. And for good reason I believe. It's not that people don't want religion. They do.
People want a religion they can *use*;
      a religion that *means* something to them,
      a religion that is *good* for them,
      a religion that helps *make sense* out of things.
They are not finding that in church anymore.

Two. Science is winning the battle for our mind. In fact, science is in our mind right now, gently feeling around and finding out the ways it works. The day is coming, in my lifetime when science will be able to say without fear of contradiction, "There is no soul here."

Which is true. It's what I've been saying.
Without a better image of God to hold up, we are reduced to being robots, computers, machines.
We are not machines. We are *vastly* more than machines.

I am proposing we re-do the image of God because we *are* the image of God. Divinity is in our selves.

53

Science and religion both seek the truth.

From a religious point of view that is also scientific (I *love* science!), I am proposing a better way to look at God, our selves, and all around us.

What's in it for you?

No hell. No devil. No purgatory. No limbo. No judgment. No sins. Not here. Not after.

No fear. No need for fear. No threat of fear. No use of fear. No fear. No Fear.

Power. We are divine. We determine reality. How much more power *is* there?

Redemption? Done.

There's no need for redemption. We are divine.

Salvation? Done.

There is nothing that needs saving. We are divine.

No complexity. No "three in one in three."

God is existence. Period.

No ancient languages. Whatever language you have is more than enough to express the God in you, the God in all, the God *of* all. Other languages are OK; they're just not necessary. The one you have is sufficient.

No ritual (unless maybe you want ritual).

No structure (unless maybe you want structure).

But no worship of words, ritual, or structure.

Death? Yes. Part of the game. Sorry.

More on that, in two chapters.

In the old way of thinking about God, divinity is strictly in God. We are sinners, doomed; we can never make it to God's level without God's help. Christians believe God sent his Son to lift us up, to die for us so that we can be one with God.

And we are. It worked! Only, we don't know it.

In the old way of thinking, we have a "physical" part that's bad and a "spiritual" part that's good.

In the better way of thinking about God, divinity is *through* us. We are far, far more beautiful than old religion portrays us. We are a connection to all that is, and if we would just allow ourselves to see it, it would become visible. God's Son is an example of how high we could rise if we would just let go of what's holding us down. We are *all* God's Sons and Daughters. More than that. We are God's expression.

In the better way of thinking, we are empowered to define ourselves. We are what we think we are.

I could go on and on about this but I've already said all I want to say in previous chapters. Go back and read the first chapter: *What We Are.*

Except this…

The world is not evil. In fact, the world is not anything at all until you say it is. Evil? Good? That's up to you. I'm going with good. Let me give you some facts to hold on to.

We are walking talking singing burping farting miracles! It takes the precise coordination of 110 muscles just to stand still! We do it every day and nobody sees it as miraculous. But it is! It's an ordinary miracle but a miracle nonetheless.

Each of us has 60,000-ish miles of blood vessels. That's 2½ times around the Earth.

We have 150 *trillion* synapses in our brain bucket. There are more synapses in *one drop* of brain tissue than there are stars in the Milky Way galaxy. Bet you *can't* wrap your head around that!

A blind person would leap for joy to be able to see! It's a miracle! We see, hear, feel, walk, and just take it all for granted. An ordinary miracle.

We are living miracles! Someday we will all know it. You're a miracle. You are a miracle.

That's what's good in all this *What.* stuff.

13. What's good?

Good and evil are easy to define. Good is what makes you happy. Evil is what takes you away from happy. There are degrees, of course. Very good things make you very happy. Little bads make you only a little unhappy.

Then it gets complicated. Something that makes you happy might make everyone else in the world not happy. That's not good.

Something that makes you happy now might make you very unhappy later. Is that good or is that bad?

The definition of "happy" varies from person to person. Lots of people are so badly hurt, so drugged out, so abused, they don't even *try* for happy; don't know happy when they see it. It can go to extremes too, as you know, where good and bad are completely reversed in someone's head.

The "Good or bad?" decision requires some thinking. Former President Lyndon Johnson once said, "Doing the right thing is not the problem. The problem is *knowing* the right thing."

But did you notice my underlying assumption in all this? Here it is: People Go for Better. Each of us tries for happy in whatever limited or large way we can; for now, and for as long as possible later. People *want* to increase love and decrease fear. When you say "I want to make a difference," everyone knows you mean "I want to make *an improvement*." It's understood.

The problem of deciding "What's good?" has been bugging humanity for forever and, as you know, we've laid down some rules and figured out some ways to live that cover a good part of the time so we don't have to do the same deciding over and over again.

Some actions are good almost all the time and some actions are bad almost all the time.
Giving is good almost all the time.
Killing is bad almost all the time.
Generally, you don't need to think those out.

But when you *do* need to think things through, look at it from the position of increasing happiness. "How do I make the most people the happiest for the longest period of time?"

You will notice, perhaps, the word "God" appears nowhere here. We don't need it. The divinity in us is enough, we don't need an external god laying down rules. *Thou* art God, bubbling up blessings through our actions all the time.

I have a friend, a very enlightened man, who ends his emails with this two-word sig: Be good.

At first glance that covers a lot. "Hey, you! Be good!"
At second glance, it covers a whole lot more. "Hey, you! You are good. Be what you are!"

Hey, we don't always go for better.
We hurt each other. We hurt ourselves.
We blindly stomp on roses with hobnail boots; sometimes purposely.

Fine. Figure it out. Fix it. In the fixing is finding God.
We're smart. We're hard-working. We can make it better.
Go for the good. I have faith in us.

14. What about Death? Part 1

We're all fascinated by death.
If it doesn't get *too close* to us.
But it's *going* to get too close to us. Every one of us.
How do we cope with that?

- We philosophize: Death is the side of life turned away from us.
- We fantasize: If you are good, when you die, you will go to heaven.
- We make jokes: Death is when your subscriptions to *Time* and *Life* expire.[16]
- We tell stories: "Momma always said, dyin' was a part of life. I sure wish it wasn't."[17]

Years ago, I had a next-door neighbor named Katherine Smith. She was 75 years old at the time. She used to mow her huge lawn every week in the hot July sun with a push mower. She was a warm and friendly little fireball of a human being. On the wall of her living room, she had a framed needlepoint. It was a picture of a simple cottage with the inscription:

> Let me live in a house
> By the side of the road
> And be a friend to man.

She told me once, "It's as natural to die as it is to be born."

I figure she should know. I have often turned to that for comfort. Maybe you can too. It's as natural to die as it is to be born.

---

[16] Thank you, George Monter.
[17] *Forrest Gump,* Winston Groom.

My best friend Larry died when he was 11. I was 7. He had "a hole in his heart" they said, and he died on the operating table when they tried to fix it. It was a long shot, they said. Since that time, I have been trying to figure out why we all have to die.

Frankly, I do not know for sure, but I have a pretty good idea. And eventually we're all going to find out. Henry Ward Beecher's[18] last words were, "Now comes the mystery!"

I had a near-death experience in my early 20's. Don't do drugs kids, they'll kill you. Suffice it to say it had all the classic symptoms of a near-death experience: the long tunnel, the bright light, the interview with God, the whole *megillah*.

And another one in my 60's. Apparently, you don't have to do drugs to have a near-death experience.

I came away from them less afraid to die. I wish I could convey the experience to you better. Maybe you could be less afraid to die too.

What does a better image of God have to say about death? Many things.

Rather than list them all, one by one, I'm going to steal a quote from my 2009 novel, *The Field*,[19] wherein our hero, Gary Cole, is having trouble sleeping.

> He tossed, turned, and did not fall asleep for what seemed like forever. He got up, twice, to pace the room and stare out the window. When he got back into bed the third time, he realized what it was. He did not want to record his dreams after all. He wanted them to be a secret, his little

[18] http://en.wikipedia.org/wiki/Henry_Ward_Beecher
[19] https://www.amazon.com/Field-story-about-future/dp/0615311172/

secret. So, he turned off the journaling and almost immediately fell into a deep sleep.

He was in the middle of the field he had seen before. The grass was green. The sky was blue. There was no sun. A fountain stood about 10 meters away, bubbling and sparkling quietly. He was not alone.

"Hey sport," said a man in an immaculate blue suit and tie. He was smiling and his eyes were the deepest eyes Gary had ever seen.

"Who are you?" said Gary, with more than a little surprise and apprehension.

"Call me God," said the same person, now a tall woman. Her blonde hair was waist-length and billowing in the breeze. "You're Gary Cole."

"Uh, yes. *God?*"

"Yes. God. You know: I Am. Allah. Nature. All power. All knowledge. Life. Truth. Love. The Preserver. The Destroyer. Beautiful. Wise. Beneficent. Merciful. The list goes on and on. 'The ground of substance and being.' I've always liked that one. You sure you want to hear them all?" Now the woman was a teen-aged boy with curly black hair, the first showings of a beard, and acne.

"No," said Gary, this time a bit steadier. "Do you have one form I could see you as?"

"Sonny-boy," said the old woman, "I *am* form. I am *all* forms. I am *what forms* form. What you're seeing is *you*, Buck-o, trying to decide what I am. You decide what I look like, Chuckles," said the old man with a smile. "And while you're doing that, I'm going to have to ask you a few questions." This time it was a police officer who spoke, in full uniform with a stylo and a pad.

"God asks questions?" said Gary. "I thought God knew everything."

"I see we've got a lot to learn here, Cutie." God was as beautiful a woman as Gary had ever seen. Her smile made him shiver, and not with the cold. "The questions aren't for me, Gary. They're for you. You do have a bit to learn. Don't fight it, just let it go." God was now a young girl with freckles, dimples, and one or two missing teeth. She was wearing a karate gi with a green belt.

"Question Number One," said the emaciated (old?) (young?) man lying on the ground. "Do you know how you got here?"

"No. And I don't even know where *here* is, or even *if* here is. Where are we, anyway?"

"Uh Uh Uhh. I'm asking the questions in this round, Skippy. You'll get your turn." God was looking a lot like Gary's eighth grade gym teacher. "And given that you don't know how you got here, I've only got one more question, and you can think about it. Don't answer now and remember, the answer is for *you*. Here's the question: 'How did you get here?'

"Now it's your turn! What can I tell you?" God was a smiling ballet dancer in a leotard and leg warmers. She was posing and stretching her legs.

Gary stopped feeling apprehensive, paused to examine this crazy situation, and with a shock realized, *he was talking to God*! And even better, *God was talking back*! He could ask her anything he wanted to know. He wanted to know what was happening to him. He wanted to know who was controlling the minds of humanity. But most of all, he wanted to know…

"What happens when we die?"

The mortician dressed in a black suit smiled. When he spoke, it was gently, kindly and with a twinkle in his eye: "You return to me."

God the old rumpled college professor continued. He laid a hand gently upon Gary's chest. "The connection between us is always on and always working. You and I are one, only you don't know it. From the moment your ears developed the ability to hear, from the moment your brain developed the ability to think; you have turned your attention to your-self."

God was now a midwife, in facemask, hospital scrubs and gloves. "At first you listened to your own heartbeat. Then you listened to your mother's heartbeat. Then your eyes started working and you haven't taken your attention off them since. And of course you should! How could you not? You are *fascinating*. *Life* is fascinating. Life is *me* and *I* am fascinating, don't you think?" said the showgirl in feathers and sequins, fluttering her eyelashes.

The monk continued. "When you've done all the living you're going to do, when you go to listen and your ears are no longer hearing, when you try to look and your eyes are closed forever, when you attempt to think and your brain isn't thinking any more, you will turn away from such things and see me again." God was Mother Nature, smiling, hugging him shoulder-to-shoulder. "And here I am! *Ta Daa!* I am always right next to you; even closer than that! And I love you! When you die," said the earth mother in sandals and waist-length hair, "you return to me."

"You make it sound like dying is something I should look forward to," said a dazed Gary.

"Nope," said God the lifeguard in red spandex. "No, no, no, and no. You are alive for a reason. Be alive. *Stay* alive. Live every moment of your life. Enjoy every sandwich.

"And yes. Don't fear the end. When you die, you don't die. The you that is you goes on.

"And I see now our time is up!" said God the smiling game show host. "Let's all give our contestant a big round of ap-plause!" and the sound of applause came from out of no-where and surrounded Gary. He felt a bit like bowing, and when he did, he shifted in bed and the applause turned into the sound of rain on his room window. He woke up. It was very early in the morning, just before sunrise.

Gary stretched, sighed, and checked his Insert. 5:34 AM. He relaxed, rubbed his face, and put his hands behind his head, grinning a little. He had talked with God! Nice dream.

He lay back, listening to the early-morning rain.

He thought, and thought, and thought; about everything, and everything, and everything.

15. What about Death? Part 2

Death scares us. Can't help it, we're built that way. It's the root of all fear. Some people go so far as to not *think* about it. Ever.

Which is a shame, because we might as well get comfortable with it. It's certain. One less worry is one more happiness.

So, what is this *death* thing that we're all so afraid of, huh?

Death is when your brain stops thinking.
Simple enough.

All the rest of our body exists to keep our brain up and running. But there is a difference between "you," and "your brain." You may already be aware of that, but if you're not, I want you to be. When your brain stops thinking, that does not mean *you* stop.

Most people think they *are* their brain, or at least they think they are *in* their brain. The brain thinks very highly of itself. The brain is magnificent. It's a natural to think we are in our brain.

But we are not our brain. We are not *in* our brain.
We are a connection to all of life.
We go *way beyond* brain. All the way to divine.
Our brain is just what we use to make the connection.

Everything goes through brain. Can't avoid it. Don't want to avoid it. Everything gets filtered, digitized, stored, and indexed by the most spectacular computer system life can create. It's usually not a problem because the system works very well.

But we're talking about death here, when the system stops. We must then talk about "you" as separate from "your brain."

What happens when the brain stops?
When you die, you don't die. The you that is you goes on.[20]
We don't die. We are still a connection to life, still divine.
Your body drops off, leaving you where you already are: connected.

Where do you go when you die?
Where you came from before you were born. You never left, actually.

Don't fear the reaper. My best friend Larry's last words were, "Daddy, I'm not afraid."

What we experience after death will be *nothing like* what we are experiencing as life.

Even the word "experience" does not apply. "Experience" is so tied to brains and thinking that even using the word is an error. We aren't going to experience *anything* if by "experience" we mean analyze and compare and judge and remember.

There are no words to describe the afterlife, so let's don't, and get rid of the ones we've used forever. No Hell. No Golden Gate. No Judgement. No Purgatory. No Limbo. No River Styx. No Angels. No harps. No Devils. No suffering. No eternal torment. No pitchforks. No wings. Nothing we can describe.

Let's enjoy the now now, and be not afraid then.

And remember this…

---

[20] Yeah, I know. Said this twice. Worth repeating.

We are not *in* our body. We are not in our brain.
We are *through* our body. We are *through* our brain.
When death takes us off the playing field, the light that passed through us, that *was* us, filters in through other paths.

For those of us who are mourning someone, the connection we knew to them is broken, that pathway is done. But the love that they expressed, the spirit that made them real, the life that they shone out into the world is still and always available. We just have to look for it in new places now, coming from new directions. Go find it.

16. Making Love

We humans express life. We are an expression of life.
If you do not know this, it is time to learn it.
If you do not think it, it is time to change your mind.
A belief is just a thought in your mind that you like to think.

But all by itself, expressing life don't amount to a hill o'beans.

What makes this "expression of life" thing important and big
and all is if we love.

Love lifts.
Without love drifts.
Gotta get to love.

What is love? Where's it come from? How's it get here?
How come there ain't more of it?

Love is our highest expression. Love is when someone else or
some*thing* else becomes more important to us than we are to
ourselves.

Love is making ourselves bigger by making what we love bigger first. Parents for children. Lovers for each other. Builders
for craft. Scientists for truth. Clerics for Truth. Homer Simpson
for beer.

It should be noted, these lines are bendable and stretchable.
Scientists also love research grants. And beer.

What makes us better than the dirt we stand on is this: we love.
We choose who, what, where, when, and how much to love.
This ability to love comes pre-installed in humans. Like hair.

What makes basketball a great game? People love watching it. What makes J. K. Rowling a great author? People love her stories.

What makes Syracuse a great place to live?

What makes love? Where's it come from?

When I was but a tender lad of 16, I fell in love for the very first time. *Ah*, first love. It was intense, *whoo*! I wrote poetry. I daydreamed. I did a lot of sighing. Love seemed to flow from me like a horse with a head cold. It took me years and years to get over her.

What makes love? I'll tell you. It's *us*, baby.
You, me, Bobby McGee.
Me, you, Mr. Magoo.
All of us what rides the bus.
Here and there and everywhere.
We make love.

There is a mechanism inside of us that generates love. We decide whom and what we will love, we make the love, and we ooze it out like toothpaste. It takes less time to do it than it takes to describe. See something you love? We love it!

All you have to do is get your fear out of the way and the love flows without stopping, like *Fast and Furious* sequels.[21]

People will tell you "All love is from God" without knowing that isn't quite true. People sincerely love all the time with no understanding, knowledge, or sense of God. In fact, the fear and close-mindedness that sometimes passes itself off as

---

[21] As of this writing, one original movie and *nine* sequels.

"God's law" limits love. Sometimes it seems in order to love, it is better to *not* know God.

That's sad. That's like saying in order to rite, its beter to nott noe howe to spel.

Yes, God is the source of love! *Of course* God is the source of love! God is the source of *everything.*[22]
If you know what God is!
The deep place in us where love is made is the "God-in-us," the God in us. God is love *through* us.

People think: "Us," "God," "separate."

Better, think: GodInUsInGod.

So, what's the point of all this poetic pouting?

If there is going to be love in the world, and there damn well *better* be love in the world, we is the ones what's got to *make* it.[23] It doesn't get into the world unless we open the door and let it in. We have to be open to love; we have to make love.

If we are not there to open the door, it doesn't go through.
If we are not there to make it, it doesn't get made.

Interestingly enough, bringing love into the world is not a necessity. We all live at least parts of our lives in a state of loveless drift. Sad.
Worse, some *never* love. Very sad.

I wouldn't be writing this and you wouldn't be reading this if making love were easy. But being a source of love is hard work. Letting yourself learn to love is a life's labor.

---

[22] ...and every thing...
[23] I know, said *that* twice too. It is also worth repeating.

And, like anything else, practice makes better.
Here's how to be a better lover.

Start with something you already love and love it a little more.
That's like, Level 1.
Love the pure empty blue sky on a sunny day?
Love the same sky with a few clouds in it.

Love roses? Love daffodils.
Love Overwatch? Love Super Smash Bros.
Tell yourself: "Love this," and let it flow. It helps to practice.

Level 2 is taking some*body* whom you already love, and loving
them more.
…
Level 9 is loving something that smells bad.
Level 10 is loving someone who hates you.
Level 11 is loving some*one* who smells bad.
…
Level 23 is loving kale.
Level 24 is loving yourself.

Love takes practice. Practice loving.
Love takes work. Work at loving.
Save big love for when you get good at little love.
The reward is *huge*: you get to love. Take that both ways.

17. The Power of Prayer

I believe in the power of prayer.

More than that.

I *rely* on the power of prayer. Prayer is my first choice. When others turn to doctors, lawyers, therapists, I am praying. It doesn't always work, but it *almost* always does, and that's *way* good enough for me.

Pray first.
Then think/plan.
Then act.

Let me tell you the story of the best thing that ever happened to me as the result of praying.

"Sherman, set the 'WayBack' to 1985."
"Jeepers, Mr. Peabody, where are we going?"
"To Boston Massachusetts, Sherman, to see a young man meet his wife."

Picture a man of 33. Married once. It didn't work. Looking for a wife in earnest now. There are bars, dance clubs, social events with his friends, church things... He is also taking a serious amount of aerobics and dance classes, even ballet classes at a *très chic* ballet school in Copley Square.

One might think a straight man in an adult ballet class would have it made. Not so.

There are dates of course, other women, women who are friends, but nothing really special. And it weighs heavily on the man. It is not like he isn't trying, but something is missing. Something is wrong and he does not know what it is.

So, he decides to start a really serious prayer effort. Pray in the morning. Pray before lunch. Pray before bed like his mother used to make him do when he was 5. Pray when driving. Pray when daydreaming. Pray when a song comes on the radio he doesn't like. Pray.

He figures, "What have I got to lose? Being single is the biggest problem I have and prayer is the strongest weapon I have." At first he doesn't even know what to pray for, so he decides to pray for what to pray for. He didn't know he could do that, until just then.

Almost immediately, what people used to call "advice to the lovelorn" starts showing up in his life. Magazine articles pop up on newsstands. A few lines in a Shakespeare play catch his attention. Married friends invite him over to their houses for dinner.

No answers, but the cauldron is beginning to bubble. That is an interesting observation.

One of the magazine articles has a particularly notable piece of advice. It says in essence, "The reason things are the way they are is because you are doing things to make them that way. Fix you."

This advice sticks with the man. It is a powerful point of view. He can control and fix *himself* if he is the problem. He hadn't even thought there was anything wrong or missing in him, so that becomes the prayer. "What am I doing to sabotage my love life?" "Show me the way up and outta here." "Show me that I am complete."

A couple weeks later the man is walking along the sidewalk, praying and thinking about his favorite topic when he flashes on a problem. He sees that although he knows he could be a good father, he does not think he is a good husband. After all, his first marriage blew apart! What kind of a husband does that make him?

So, now he prays about being a good husband. He looks up the word "husband" in the dictionary and it says "husband" comes from two words: "hus," which means "house," and "band," which means "to hold." A husband is a "house-holder."

So, then the prayer becomes, "Help me to see that I am a good house-holder."

In a couple of days, he knows that he is. It's clear. This is on a Thursday.

On Saturday he meets her.

True story.

18. What about Soul?

A man climbs Mt. Sinai in order to talk to God.
Looking up, the man says, "God, what does a million years mean to you?"
God replies, "A minute."
The man then asks, "And what does a million dollars mean to you?"
God replies, "A penny."
Then the man asks, "Can I have a penny?"
God replies, "In a minute."

The one and only reason we believe in a "soul" is because dying is so scary. A soul that dwells in the body, breaks out at death, and lives on after death makes dying bearable. The soul goes to heaven, death isn't final. There's real comfort in that: life after death.

But it's a story, a myth, a fable we tell ourselves to comfort ourselves in real pain.

Here's a new story.

We are connected to all that is. We are an example of life. We and life are one, not separate, not separable. Life goes on when you die. So do you. The you that is really you, that is. What you really are is a connection.

I am not so naïve as to believe I can reverse a cultural norm as strong as the idea that there's a soul dwelling inside the body. But I gots to say what I gots to say. There is no soul inside your body. Period. Rather, the opposite is closer to the truth. We are all inside soul.

It is easy to see how this idea of a soul inside the body got started. Our brain contains our name, our memories, our sense of what is real, our sense of who we are, what we are, where we are. How the brain works is mysterious, up until now, anyway. It's easy to give it a magical quality. And remember, just because we can understand and explain it does not make it any less divine.

If we want to be unlimited, or at least *less* limited, reverse the idea that there is a soul inside us. We are in soul. Swim in it. Surrender to life. It's got us surrounded. *Let* it surround you. Be in life. Be of life. Let life pass through you. Everyone does this at least a little bit anyway. Be aware of the life coming through you and be open to more of it.

There is a series of very popular books entitled *Chicken Soup for the Soul*. I love chicken soup, but this is an example of the problem. Soul doesn't need chicken soup. What we think of as soul is really brain. It's brain that needs the chicken soup, but that would make a terrible book title.

It is very important to understand that what we think of as soul is really brain. It makes your innermost thoughts and mysterious feelings more accessible when they are located inside your head rather than outside your thinking in some kind of soul thing. Removing soul puts you closer in touch with your you. That cannot be a bad thing.

Don't put soul in you.
Put you in soul and you will be closer to the truth.

Pass the chicken soup.

19. What about Forgiveness?

We are connections to God. We are connected *to* God. If our connection is weak and could be brighter (and whose isn't?), how do we build a better, brighter connection?

At the beginning of the service where I go to church on Sunday, the Pastor starts the service with a declaration of forgiveness. "As a called and ordained minister," he says, "I declare to you the entire forgiveness of all your sins."

I like that. Always have. Very reassuring.
But I tell you, it's not enough. Necessary, but not sufficient.

Don Henley with others wrote and recorded a song in 1989 entitled *The Heart of the Matter* with these words:

> I've been tryin' to get down to the heart of the matter
> But my will gets weak and my thoughts seem to scatter
> But I think it's about...forgiveness
> Forgiveness

Again, close.

Forgiveness is not about God forgiving us.
Forgiveness *has never been* about God forgiving us. You cannot hurt God. You cannot "put things right" with God.
They already are.
Forgiveness is *us* forgiving *us*.

The words of forgiveness and blessing spoken by clerics all over the world every day, are there to tell us, "Wipe your slate clean, buck-o. You're carrying too much baggage."

As a seven-year-old Catholic boy, I made my first Confession. I don't know exactly how many sins a seven-year-old can accumulate: stealing, lying, getting angry; but I know I scoured my memory and told that priest every bad thing I could remember I had ever done. I made a good Act of Contrition, said my penance, and God Forgave Me! When I walked out of that church on that Saturday morning, I was 10 feet off the ground! I was light, floating, released! The power of forgiveness! I did not understand it then. I do now.

I was mistaken. God had not forgiven me. *I* had forgiven me. God is not like us. God does not keep score. There are only two people keeping score of our mistakes. Us, and the people we hurt. Let's do the far more neglected one first: us hurting us.

We Hurt Us

When we do something wrong, in order to keep going, we have to tell ourselves it wasn't wrong, and then not think about it. Lots of things wrong means lots of things we cannot think about. Lots of things we can't think about means a smaller us. That's a hurt. When we do wrong, we hurt us. That's what makes it wrong.

Feeling forgiven frees up those places we can't think about. That's the lightness, the floating, the release; we're open again! That's what happened to me at the age of seven:
I forgave myself.

There is one big problem with me sitting here telling you to forgive yourself and that's this: I have no idea how you're going to do it.

Everybody's different. Some people are guilty. Some people are ashamed. Some people are neglected. Some people overcompensate. Some people are just scared. I have no idea what

78

it's going to take for you to feel better, but I can tell you this: You want happy in two words?
Here they are: Forgive Yourself.

To forgive yourself is to love yourself, the hardest thing in the world to do. It takes *work*. Somewhere, somehow, some way, love yourself; even if it's only a little bit. Find something about you that's loveable and love it. Get that wedge in the door and keep it there. If you can pry up a small corner of the scab, you will eventually pick off the whole thing. Underneath is healing.

Forgiveness is giving up all hope for a better past.

Be *nice* to yourself. Be *kind* to yourself. Be *gentle* on yourself. Unconditionally. Listen to your voices criticizing you and re-alize that even the most critical, angry, ugly, *awful* inner voice is trying to help you. Trying to help.
A great idea: just poorly implemented.

It's okay to share your frustration with self-forgiveness if you need to. Anybody who knows you well will be astonished if you start a conversation with, "I'm having a bit of trouble ac-cepting myself today." Kicks the whole conversation up a notch, don't it?

But back to what I said seven paragraphs ago. I have no idea how you're going to forgive yourself; I just know that if you want better, you *must* forgive yourself. Not beg God for for-giveness; beg *yourself* for forgiveness. Totally cuts out the middle man. Allow yourself to feel forgiven. You were a kid, what the hell did *you* know? You made a mistake. You had to do it the wrong way to learn to do it the right way. Pick up the pieces, say "I'm sorry" to yourself, smile, and get on with your life.

We Hurt Others

Next, the really messy problem of gathering forgiveness from the people we have hurt. Sure are a lot of them, aren't there? Too many to count in one sitting probably. Better make a list.

I have a list. I try to keep it as short as possible. I had a name on my list from 1971. I insulted someone who might have been my friend but for my loose cannon of a mouth. In 2009 I had a chance to apologize to him and I did. It felt *wonderful*! Thirty-eight years! Longer than it takes to make a good bottle of scotch! Burden: gone!

Notice: they do not have to forgive you. That's their burden. Make it right as best you can. They do not have to accept your sincere apology. You do not have to get them to.

Also know there are many things we have done that cannot be un-done. That brings us back to Forgive Yourself. Carrying the burden of an un-fixable mistake is like carrying a whole other person on your shoulders. If we can't fix it, put it down.
Make it right as best you can and stop punishing yourself.

If you need to pray to feel forgiven, go right ahead and pray. Just remember, God is *in* you. The seat of divinity is not in some far-off heaven. The seat of divinity is wearing your socks and shoes right now. Pray to God-in-you, let God have it. Forgive yourself. You are forgiven.

"Your Sins Are Forgiven"

Anyone who tells you your sins are forgiven is both doing you a favor and harming you at the same time. They're encouraging you, and supporting the myth. The concept of sin was created to scare people into obeying. It has done that job for forever. Not any more. Sin doesn't work. It only makes people angry.

Time to be a grownup. There is no sin, only better and worse.
God does not hold a grudge, but you do.
Put it down.
Love more. Fear less.
Fear less. Love more.
Forgive yourself. Ask others to forgive you.
That's the hard work. Do the hard work.

20. What about Healing?

Any religious practice that doesn't lead to healing is just an intellectual exercise. Not bad, but how much time do you have to spend on only theory?

The proof of the pudding is in the eating.
The proof of the thinking is in the healing.
If you group together a bunch of ideas from previous chapters, you get a mental foundation for healing. Let me spell it out for you here in this chapter.

First, a definition of terms.
This is healing, not "spiritual healing." Healing is when you get better. Spiritual healing is, well, I'm not sure I know what spiritual healing is. "Spiritual" and "physical" are a false dichotomy. Physical is spiritual. Spiritual is physical. We are one *mindbodyspirit*, not mind, body, and spirit.

Second, the goal is healing, not holier-than-thou. I have no problem with doctors. In fact, I carry my mental bag of healing ideas with me whenever I go to the doctor. The tools help me seek out and find doctors who are healers and avoid doctors who are mechanics.

Third, I be talkin' 'bout *you* healing you, not *me* healing you. I have had only four cases of me healing someone other than myself, and they were all in my immediate family. I'm not yet far enough along in my learning to heal at a distance. The principles do apply though, and I'm sure distance healing with these principles is possible.

And anyway, you need to do your own healing for a few very good reasons. You are the best person to heal you. You know the problem. You will find the solution. Hell, you may even *be* the problem. Who better to heal you than you?

Now we begin. There are three steps.

Step 1: You Can Heal.

Reality is what you accept as real: accept the reality of healing. Healing is possible. You can heal. If any part, any *little* part of you is saying "I can't heal," or "I can't heal myself," or "I can't be healed," you're right. Cannot have that. Stop stopping yourself from healing. You can be healed. You can heal yourself. You can heal. The nature of Nature is to heal.
Got to have it. Say it. Know it.

If "I can heal" is too strong a stance for you, take a step back and try: "Healing is nearby. I am open to it." Start there. Work yourself up to "I can heal." Prayer helps.

Open yourself up to the reality that you can heal, and you can be healed. That's Step 1 and you must have it.

Step 2: Find the Part That's Afraid.

Let's take the time in 2000 when I threw my back out for the very first time. My little 4-year-old ran towards me and jumped into my arms. I caught him like I always did, but this time something inside went "*Oh!*"

I didn't think much about it that day or the morning of the next, but by the afternoon I was in more pain that I have ever felt. I could not walk. I could not stand. I could not sit. I learned that I have a point where I will do *anything* to relieve the pain. My wife laid a few blankets on the living room floor for me and I lived there for days by the care of my wife and family.

The turning point was late in the night of the 2nd night on the floor. I was desperate. I did not know if I would ever walk again. I did something desperate. "The gift of desperation."

I took a mental walk into my brain, down my spine, through my nerves, and poked around until I found the spot in my back that was giving me the most pain.

What I found was a very frightened muscle, very much afraid I had injured my spine, and hell-bent on keeping my spine from ever moving again so that I couldn't hurt it.

I had a mental conversation with that muscle; listening to how afraid it was, and I reassured it that indeed my spine was intact and uninjured. I tried to be soothing, gentle; in other words: loving.

Step 3: Love it.

My pain turned the corner. I started feeling less bad from that moment. I knew I had done something by loving the part that was afraid.

It may look like blood, or a torn muscle, or something elaborate and complicated like a spot on an ultrasound. But somewhere, at the root of the problem, is fear that needs to be loved.

We *have* to be loving to our body. We have to be loving *with* our body. Our body is not as quick as we are. It doesn't "get" nuance. It doesn't respond to "like." It doesn't understand "clever." It knows love. It feels love. It responds to love.
Just like you do.
Give it love.

Those are the steps.

I did not state, and I do not mean to imply, that any part of this is easy. It is not. It is very difficult. Every "step" could be called a "milestone."

Let me amend that. *I* find every step difficult. Your mileage may vary.

And there are traps and smokescreens and self-deceptions all along the way.
For one thing, finding the part that's scared is scary. It is frightening to find the frightened part. Does that make sense?

Parts of you will scream "It's not my fault!"
or
"It's *X*'s fault!" where here you fill in the name of the current blame leader (or blame situation). That's a smokescreen.

You may convince yourself you're not afraid. You may feel it very deeply. But is some part of you broken? Then some part of you is afraid. It may not be the part that is hurting. Hurt is a cry for help caused by fear, but hurt and fear are two different things.
Our job is to find the part that's *afraid*, not the part that hurts.

Or the hurt may be gone. The fear is not. Start with where you are or were hurting and look around. The fear is afraid of being found. You can probably understand that. It is difficult to face your fear.

Remember "I'm Responsible" back in chapter 11? Taking the responsibility for the disease, the injury, the complaint, the problem, gives you the power to fix it.

Pushing the fault away onto something or someone else may feel good temporarily. It may even give you a feeling of righteousness. But, do you want to *appease* the hurt, or do you want to *heal* it? How long do you want to be in pain?

Healing with love is a human superpower.
We can make love, and give it away, and that heals.

And don't think "miracle." Don't you *dare* go there. Or better, if you have to think miracle, think "ordinary miracle."

We are surrounded by miracles. Miracles are freaking commonplace. We call them "childbirth," or "eyesight," or "thinking," or "hearing," or even "walking," and we just take them for granted. It's time to realize we take miracles for granted.

They're ordinary miracles, Bob.[24] We are divine.
If only we knew it better.

And don't forget there is a huge human tradition for this kind of healing. Sit quietly through any Alcoholics Anonymous meeting and you're likely to hear more than one healing story, and they don't call them miracles in AA.[25]

Calling them "miracles" is an estrangement, an unearned glorification. Nobody is comfortable with miracles, even though miracles can happen at any time with absolutely no warning. Come out of the clouds, healer.

Let me tell you about a healing using this technique, that I did last Saturday.[26]

I injured my Achilles tendon near the ankle of my right leg months ago. I don't remember when it happened, only that the first I was aware of it, I had to be very careful going down stairs because it hurt, every step. It was a constant low level of pain

---

[24] Who's Bob?
[25] They call them "a moment of clarity," or "a spiritual understanding."
[26] October, 2013. I *told* you this book sat on my hard drive for a long time.

and occasionally, especially in the morning, awful. We're talking since April, and this was October.

I'm the guy who heals himself.
Why didn't I do something about it?

Well, I tried.
I'm still learning.

I've got the principles, and I'm giving the principles to you, but as professors of mine in college used to say, "The details are left as an exercise for the interested student." I am still a student.

At first, I loved my leg, my ankle, my calf. It felt a little better, but it didn't go away. I thought I remembered when I injured it: someone banged me with their shopping cart at Costco I thought, and that made me feel a little better because then I wasn't responsible. But that was a diversion (a smokescreen) and the pain did not go away.

Recently the pain inched up just past the point where it pissed me off. That was last Saturday, like I said.

I sat down with my right leg crossed over my left and I felt around with my fingers for the spot that hurt the very worst. I found it and *boy* did it hurt when I did! However, I did not back off against the fear. I made love in my heart for my Achilles tendon and I sent that love into my fingers. I felt something go *goosh* in the spot that hurt and I knew something had healed. The rest of the day I occasionally touched it again and smiled at it mentally, trying to let it know that I sincerely loved my Achilles tendon. After all, it is the part that makes the whole walking thing possible.

I did the same thing the next day, first thing in the morning before I got out of bed. I assured my poor, slow-to-realize Achilles tendon that I truly and indeed loved it with a deep and sincere love. Some parts of your body take more assurance than others, or they have to hear the story more than once or twice before they believe it. Kinda like us.

Anyway, the capper of this story is, I zoomed down the stairs yesterday noon on the way to the car and I realized, half-way down, that I have not done that in more than a season! I am willing to admit that my tendon is healed. I am also willing to give my tendon more assurance that it is loved, if it needs it.

To re-cap:
> Know that you can heal.
> Find the part that is frightened.[27]
> Love it.[28]
> Repeat as necessary.

As you are loving the frightened spot, it may recede and another frightened spot will become visible. This is OK. You're still finding *the* frightened spot. Love it. Repeat as necessary.

Be very careful whom you tell about your healing. Others' doubts can cause you to doubt, and the fear will return. Guard against relapse and should one occur, remember that you can use the same tools to re-heal. It's just fear.

These steps can be difficult, nearly impossible. Doctors have to go to school for what, eight years, and three years of Residency to learn to be healers? Me, I had to get desperate, or really angry, to finally get up the gumption to find the fear and heal myself.

---

[27] Find the *parts* that *are* frightened.
[28] Love *them*.

Do not give up. I have faith in you. We are divine. The nature of nature is to heal. And if the pain gets bad enough, that is, if the cry for love gets loud enough, you will respond. We always do. We are human. It is our goal to learn, to love, to heal.

21. Whupside-Down

I have a friend whose mother tried to kill her, twice; when she was about twelve.

Her grandparents stepped in and separated daughter from mother, took the girl into their home, and raised her like their very own child in a loving, safe household.

Clearly Mommy Dearest was *way* off her nut, but how do you explain that to a child?

I'm pretty sure you don't. And consequently, my friend grew up looking for, and never finding, love from her mother.

That kind of thing hurts you. Deeply. Not having mother-love is an enormous problem to overcome. It leaves a huge hole. Everybody needs approval, acceptance, and *unconditional love* at an early age. Everybody.

Not getting it sets up a certain set of beliefs, assumptions in your mind, and that bends the rest of your life in a particular direction. A part of you just feels *empty* for ever. We arrive at the totally illogical logical conclusion: "If my own *mother* didn't love me, *nobody* is ever going to love me."

And what you believe about yourself *becomes* yourself. Reality is what you accept as real. It is so sad and screwed-up and unnecessary when we accept wrong.

But "Reality is what you accept as real" can work *for* you too. Let us begin to heal. Challenge the bad assumptions and set about building a better set of beliefs.

First, all the love you need; all the love you want; all the love you could ever hold is lying in wait inside of you, waiting for you to make it. John Lennon had it right but let me say it another way: all you need is *to* love.

Children whose parents loved them unconditionally were given more than love; they were given an *example* of loving. These children have a wordless understanding that they too can love unconditionally: they've seen it done.

What do you do if you don't have an example of unconditional love in your life to work from? Make one up! It's easier than learning to ride a bicycle! It takes practice, repetition, and you must get back up on the bike every time you fall. But loving is much more natural to us than riding a bicycle.

And it doesn't require a bicycle! :-)

In 7th grade, my family moved and I was dropped into a new school. I was *fiercely* lonely. My father gave me some advice when he finally got tired of listening to me moan and groan about how the kids in northern Virginia were so different from the kids in southern Virginia: "They're unfriendly. They're petty. They talk about you behind your back. They…"

He shut me up with, "If you want a friend, *be* a friend."
He was totally right.

And I didn't know until much later in life that his statement is a small piece of a much larger life rule.

To my friend with the damaged mother and anyone else reading this who never got enough mother-love I say: if you *want* unconditional love and acceptance, *give* unconditional love and acceptance. It works. Period.

Open the last gate. Turn off the last safety valve. Love with reckless abandon. Love like you've never been hurt. Love first.

The world is built upside-down. We think our beliefs are based on our experiences, but it works exactly the opposite of that.

Our experiences are based on our beliefs.
Believing is seeing. Act as if. You find what you look for.
Living like there *is* unconditional love in the world makes it *become true* in your life.
Love *yourself* unconditionally. (Do that first!)

Some people would call this "fake it 'till you make it."

Maybe so, but I like to say: If you want it, Give It.

If you want it
      and you give it,
            you'll get it.

22. An 8th Step Up

Earlier in this book I wrote "What's Up?" Fourteen words to higher.

I want to add two more words.

You may recall, but probably not, that at that time I wanted to glorify you, to convince you that you are something special, worth-while, hot snot.

And at the time I wrote, "Can't do that without your help." Which is true. You are in charge of you.

I want to help you feel better.
Follow along with me as I try to build a logical progression.

We are divine, an expression of life. We are as bright and expressive of the light of life as we allow ourselves to be. Which would be great except it also goes against us. We limit ourselves. We are so powerful we can limit our power. Nobody is free from this. Good or bad, the way we think about our *us* defines us. The way to improve our selves, the way to feel better, is to improve the way we hold our self in mind. You are the only barrier between God and you.

I have several times summarized these previous 94 words with these 7 words: Reality is what you accept as real.

Happily, we are trainable. Actions lead the brain into right thinking much more surely than thinking leads the brain into right action. Act as if. That's the way it works best.

The "What's up?" chapter was an attempt to list seven things to do that will lead you to thinking better about you.

Now here's an eighth one.

In addition to Be Grateful, Equal Beings, Fear Teaches, I'm Responsible, Love Yourself, No Resistance, and See Love, there's one more:

Serve Somebody

Not full time; not slavery, but on a schedule, go out and do something for somebody for free. If it's the right something and the right somebody, you will feel *wonderful* for doing it.

This is why it's imperative we help the poor. Not because it helps them (which it does) but because *it helps us*. And it will be a valid feeling. That kind of thinking will seep into you, and eventually in your deepest darkest cave of self-hatred, your tiny voice will speak to the Grumbly dwelling there and say, "Grumbly! I am a Grade-A double-plus 24-karat exalted honking *good person*!" And it will be true.

It does not make logical sense that giving something away is good for you, but it is. If logic were enough to explain everything, we'd be done already.

Serve Somebody. It makes you good.

23. What Does "Connected" Mean?

When I was 18 years old, my father packed me and my belongings in the car and drove me off to college. It took us two days to drive from Chicago and upon arriving in Cambridge, Massachusetts we stayed in a Holiday Inn.

It is important to this story that you know that I look, sound, stand, act, and think a lot like my father did. My father was my model. I know a lot of people did not get a model in their lives. I did.

That night, my father and I shared a double room in that Holiday Inn. At some point in the evening, he stepped out of the bathroom into the main room clad in his bath towel. At eighteen, I was still on my way up, had not yet attained my physical peak. My father was 48 then, well past-peak and in one glance I knew: *I could not possibly have come from this man.*

That thought bothered me for decades. How could it be? He was my *father*, no doubt about it. But I came from *that*?! I am spirit. I am creativity. I am life. What I am could not possibly have come from him. Sorry Pops, I didn't come from you.

And it's true and it took me decades to figure it out.
When I did, it was a shock, a humbling shock.

We are not the source of life. We are not the source of creativity. We are not the source. Something else; call it life, soul, spirit, higher power, God, creator; *something else* animates us.

We are a pathway. It comes *out* of us, but it doesn't start *in* us.

Not *from* us; *through* us.

I'm fine with it now but it took a while for my brain to stop being angry that it was not The Source. It's not. And I come here not *from* my father, but *through* my father. My children too: not from me; through me.

I have discovered that once I get my self out of the way, the creativity flows much better.

And the best part?! Being a pathway to spirit, life, and creativity is a bitchen[29] thing to be!

The idea is scalable. What applies to you, and me, applies to every living thing.

Bigger than that. What applies to me and you and every living thing applies to everything and all and every thing. To a greater or lesser extent, every tiny shimmer of existence is a pathway from-and-to essence / spirit / soul / creativity / *blahblahblah* whatever it is you want to call it: God.

If you're finding that hard to follow, just go back to "Not from me; through me." If you've got it, I've just saved you 30 years of figuring-it-out. You're welcome.

But that's *500 words*! Too long! How can I say it in a sound bite?

What we are is *a connection to* something.
Life is that something. We are a connection to life.

So, Pops; Mom too: thank you.

---

[29] California 1970's jargon. Good, great, fantabulous.

24. Connection Communication Communion

We live in a connected world. We cannot *live* without our cell phones. I walked past a bus stop in Porter Square the other night and nine out of the eleven people standing there were staring at their cell phones.

We cannot live without our cell phones because they connect us to each other.
Every connection is a form of communication.
Communication, with love, is a form of Communion.
Connection leads to Communication leads to Communion.
We vitally need those 3 C's. The light is connecting to itself.

But!

We live in a separated world. We walk in the world and separate ourselves from it. We "don't-see" almost all of what's around us.

There may be a better word for "don't-see."
"Ignore," or "filter," or "delete," maybe.
Don't-see is an active thing, and we do it all the time.
Let me give an example.

I used to own a Nissan car. It was coming time to replace it and my garage mechanic recommended I take a look at the Toyota Camry.

"Camry? What's a Camry?"

Right after that I was amazed to see Camrys everywhere I looked, everywhere I drove: Camrys! The Camry was the most popular car in America!

And I didn't even *see* them.
Before I was made aware, I missed a huge amount of data.
Afterwards, there were Camrys everywhere including Camry look-alikes from Honda, Nissan, and Ford. Where had I been? Nowhere. I was just not-seeing. And we all do it. All the time.

What I want to do here is make you aware of something really big that is getting not-seen.

Remember we are all expressions of life, expressions of God, but this time I want to go in the opposite direction. Instead of starting from the light inside us shining outwards, I want to start from "out," and go "in."

The light shining out *through* us is a connection *to* us too. God is connected to you. That connection goes in both directions. We are connected to God, God is connected to us.

It goes one step further:
We are connected to life. Everyone else is connected to life.
We are connected to everyone else.
We cannot be alone.
But we can *feel* alone. We can feel disconnected.
Or rather like me and the Camrys, connected but unaware of it. And frankly Frank, that's the same thing.

To be connected to life and *unaware* of it is a huge hole.
Wake up!
It's like playing basketball in high heels. Sure, it can be done, but what a hindrance!

Being aware of our "connectedness" makes us more of what we are. We become bigger than our body; we become a community.

You are connected, through you, to life. This is a fact. It is a physical hold-it-in-your-hands-and-look-at-it *fact*. Let me talk about that for a couple of paragraphs. We and the world are connected in many ways. In addition to our eyes and our ears, I want to talk about three other ways.

One. The Skin.

The first connection from outside is through our skin. It's on the outside, *duh*. It's the first and most obvious way. The world touches us through the skin and vice-versa.

But the surface area of a human being is small. Even if every inch of our skin is feeling connected, that's only maybe 2 square yards? A patch, but a start.

Two. The Lungs.

Then there's the lungs, the second way life touches us. Huge. All those tiny little blood vessels that touch the air have an area of about 100 square yards; half a tennis court! *That's* a connection baby: through the lungs!

Three. The Brain.

But hang on! The third way makes the other two fade away by comparison. The brain! The brain! We have 86 billion[30] neurons, each of which are connected to 10 to 10,000 [31] other neurons through "synapses." These synapses from neuron-to-

---

[30] -ish
[31] -ish

neuron are really not connections at all. Our neurons do not touch. Instead, there are tiny gaps with electro-chemical reactions going on in the gaps. Our brain is doing chemistry, physics, and quantum physics in *hundreds of trillions* of places.

We are an octopus with *150 trillion* tentacles;
each one gently touching the essence of existence.
That's a connection, baby!

Do you have skin? Do you have lungs? Do you have a brain?
You are *deeply* connected to life.
I rest my case.

If you want to feel your connection to life,
your connection to God,
and I Want You To,
take ahold of these three ways and feel connected to God.

Start with the skin. Reach outwards through your body. Feel the outdoors, the warmth, the cold, the wind, the rain, the sun, the moon, the stars. Be comfortable where you are. That's life. Through your skin.

Next, quiet down and just think about your breathing.
Feel the air going slowly in and out of you.
In. (*I'm alive!*)
And out. (*I release myself!*)
Feel the life within you, flowing fast, flowing slow.
Moving.
And being still.
Moving.
And being still.
That's life.
Through your lungs.

Now go to the top of your being and know you are one in life; one in God. Life is within you. You are in life.

Watch the creative being that you are be creative.

Invent a combination of things never done before, never seen before. That's your connection to the all-ness of life. That's your brain grabbing pieces of *allness*. We use it and rely on it all the time.

Speak a sentence that's never been spoken before,
Figure out how to quickly get across town at rush-hour,
Figure out how to get enough water to Los Angeles,
Figure out how to get people who hate (fear) each other to sit still and listen to each other.
That's life.
Through your brain.

Old God-images would have us believe that God is in His Heaven and we are all poor suffering *schlubs* down on Earth.
No. That's *entity* God.

I'm proclaiming to you: *existence God.*
We need this better understanding desperately!
We are *next* to God. Closer than that! *In* God.

It's all about the connection. We are in God and God is in us.
At every level we are connected to God.
And each other.
And everything.
And all.
And every thing.
You cannot be alone.
Connection. Communication. Communion.
Can't get away from it.
Reach out and feel for it.
You will find it.

25. What Is "Is"?

Bigger than Reality

Principal Poop is addressing the pep rally at his Communist Martyrs High School. The restless audience of students is heckling him mercilessly for everything he says. He continues on gamely, ineptly. At one point mid-way through his address, an un-named student in the audience shouts out in desperation, "*What is reality*?!"
The principal ignores the question, of course.

This moment in The Firesign Theatre's 1970 record album *Don't Crush That Dwarf*... is a bruising satire of education in America, saying basically "Our schools have all kinds of answers to questions the students don't have, but no answers at all to the questions they *do* have."

One learns to just not ask questions like, "What is reality?"
I believe I have answered that question.
Reality is what you accept as real.

There is a bigger question than "What is reality?"

We have former President Bill Clinton to thank for popularizing it. Some people say it was the defining moment of his Presidency. His statement, "It depends on what the meaning of the word 'is'...is," opened the door to asking what I believe is the ultimate question:

What is "is"?

So, let's take a stab at it, shall we?

Define the Universe

There are a whole bunch of absolutes in this universe of ours. To name five, there's the speed of light, Planck's constant, the gravitational constant, the Euler number, and Pi.[32]

Science has given all these values single-letter names: c, h, G, e, and π. These values are so fundamental, so often used, so *everywhere*, that using more than one letter to write them down would be a waste of space.

Take Einstein's famous **E=mc²** equation, with the value of **c²** (the speed of light, squared) fully written out:

```
E = m 89,875,517,873,681,764 Joules per kilogram
```

Kinda doesn't have the same *snappiness* as **E=mc²**, does it?

Years ago, there was a bogus college final exam floating around MIT that poked fun at how absurdly difficult MIT was. I remember two questions from that exam. One was:

Transform lead into gold. Show all work.

The other one I remember, the last question on the exam, for Extra Credit, was:

Define the universe. Give three examples.

I didn't know it at the time but it turns out that's an easy question to answer.

A decent definition of the universe can be composed by simply listing the five absolutes above (with maybe a few more) and

---

[32] Look 'em up! Wikipedia is your friend!

then saying, "The Universe is what you get when π equals 3.14159, e equals 2.71828, G equals…"

The "give three examples" part is easy too. Just twiddle the values and describe the universe that results. For example, what would the universe look like if the value of π were 1? [33]

Sorry. I'm being a nerd. I am a nerd.
I will try to make myself clear here.

Our universe is measurable, has structure, consistency, and repeatability. In other words, our universe *is*.
This does not define "is," but it does give us one example.

What Do We Know?

Knowledge, what we know, is a web of relationships of one thing to the next thing. Nothing stands alone. Everything everyone "knows" is expressed in terms of something else that they also *know*.

Take for example this fact:
Carson City is the capital of Nevada.

To "know" this, one must know what a "capital" is, what a "Nevada" is, and what a "city" is.

A "capital" is a city where the offices of government are located.
A "Nevada" is a state in The United States of America.
A "government" is a system to administer laws.
A "state" is a geographic and political portion of a country.
A "United States of America" is a country on Earth in the Western hemi…
A "city" is…

---

[33] Answer: all circles would be lines.

An "office" is…

See how it turns into a *web* of relationships very quickly? Nothing stands alone. Everything is defined by its relationship to something else, which is defined by its relationship to something else, which…

The absolutes of the universe are part of the web too. The speed of light for example needs "distance" and "time" in order to make sense.

It is the *relationship* that makes something "make sense." Something makes sense because of how it relates to the other things around it. Every thing is like that.

How Much Do We Know?

"Knowing" something does not mean you have *all* the relationships in all directions. In fact, a lot of what we know is based on only a few connections to other ideas, with the rest left unexplored. We don't need to know something in its *every* detail in order to work it and use it.

Take electrical engineering for example, my college major. I could make circuits work, and design pieces of computers, but do not ask me what an electron is. I was an *electrical* engineer, I studied *electronics*, yet the electron, the fundamental building block of electronics, is a total mystery to me. I have never actually seen an electron. All I need to know is that it exists and acts in a certain way. What it "is" is unimportant. A few months ago, I learned that an electron doesn't seem to have a size! It has weight, and charge, but no size! And you know what? I don't care! I don't ever need to know that!
But it is a fun fact and I love fun facts! :-)

We don't need to know everything to work the world. A few facts will suffice and the rest we can assume. And we do. Thomas Edison summed it up a century ago when he said, "We don't know one ten-millionth of one percent of anything." Not knowing everything has not stopped us.[34]

So?

What humanity is doing is fleshing out the web of existence. We're finding out how one thing relates to another, to another... We're playing *Six Degrees of Kevin Bacon*[35] with existence. What something *is* is how it relates to the other things it is connected to. "Capital" connects to "city" connects to "state" connects to "country" connects to...

What about the web itself? What does the whole web connect to? Turns out we have a name for that too: God.

The whole web connects to God.

God is is.

Kinda cool, ain't it?

---

[34] In fact, in attempting to define the word "is" I have used it 53 times. That's why we laughed at Bill Clinton. Everybody already knows what the meaning of the word "is" is, right? ;-)

[35] A game, based on the idea that *any* two actors in the world are connected by no more than six intermediate other actors, one of whom is actor Kevin Bacon.

26. God is *Lots* of Things

In 2020 when I first wrote this book, I was hoping to *guide* people to change their image of God. I'm older now, wiser, humbler. The error of my ways is clear to me now. Don't *change* your image of God, open it up, add to it.

God is big. Bigger than that. The human brain has a hard time holding so much *stuff* and even contradictory things, at the same time. Not impossible, but not easy. And that's exactly what I'm asking you to do. Simply put, God is lots of things.

There is a Christian image of God.
There is a Jewish image of God.
There is a Hindu image of Gods.
There is a Moslem image of Allah.
There is a Buddhist image of not God.
There is an Atheist image of no God.
There is an Agnostic image of don't know God.

All these images are alive in the minds of us divine, connected-to-all-of-life human beings. They are all correct for the persons holding them. God is existence, and existence is too multi-faceted to be pictured… too big to be encompassed… too much of everything to be only one thing.

God is love.
God is fear.
God is creator.
God is destroyer.
God is everything.
God is nothing.

One image is not all there is to it. Everything that is good, everything that is bad, everything that is possible, everything that *is*… is an expression of God. The time has come for humanity to up our mental game.

Instead of considering other religions and fixating on how they are wrong, different from each other; look for what we all have in common. What do Jews and Atheists have in common? Moslems and Christians? Buddhists and Agnostics?

God is not either/or. God is both/and.

Open up your hearts and minds, humanity. We're old enough to do that now.

27. God and Us

Our ideas of divinity form our models of humanity. –Mary Baker Eddy

It is not possible to state something is "better" without imply-ing right away that something else is worse. I'm sorry for that, for these are emotional topics. People do not think with their heads, they think with their hearts, and they think about *God* with their hearts most of all. There is a good reason why one should not discuss Religion and Politics with strangers.

But humanity has grown. Grown in sophistication. Grown in knowledge. Grown in ability to understand. *What.* is a better image of God. And along with that better image of God is a better image of you. And reality. I've tried to cover everything. Let me know if I've left anything out. I had to do it. Nature wants better. It's like a law or something.

Old god-models are based on an image that no longer fits the subject. Not bad; it got us this far! But it needs to be better now. The idea of "Spiritual: good; Physical: bad," just no longer ap-plies. We can understand that now. We are divine. Do you see that this is what I've been trying to say for 28,400 words? God is not big and powerful, and humanity is not small, sinful, and in need of salvation. *Stop that*! We are as divine as we allow ourselves to be! It is time to fully understand that.

What. is a better image of God-and-Us. In the old image, God is "up there" and us is "down here." Is it too much of a shock to realize that God is *with* us and we are with God?

Divinity is in us, and here, and throughout all creation. There is no separation between Creator and Creation.

We just have to look with the right eyes to see it.

What. is a method of healing, a three-part method of healing: know you can heal, find the fear, and love it. It is not a new idea but rather the central method of all progress since before words were invented. You may have heard it expressed another way: take your light and shine it into the darkness.

We can heal. I'm telling you there's magic in our minds. Some-day soon we're going to found it, surround it, and compound it. And just because you can fully understand it does not make it any less divine.

Old religion is based on a model that says humans needs to be scared into doing good. I can't speak for how humanity was 2,000 years ago, 4,000 years ago, but today, you *can't* be scared into doing good. We can only be scared into being scared, and that is not good.

What. values viewpoints. All the words of all the disciples and all the sages of all the ages are important if they lift the human being. Understanding our divinity requires it.

There is no hell, except the hell we create for ourselves. There is no need for redemption, unless we feel there is, and there it is. There is no need for somebody to intercede for us at the throne of God. We are already *on* the throne of God. God is closer to us than the air we breathe, than the thinks we think.

Is it blasphemy, heresy, apostasy to proclaim a tight bond be-tween God and God's creation? A oneness? A better under-standing of the relationship between God and us? I don't think so. We are *all* "seated at the right hand of The Father," and don't let anyone tell you otherwise. Especially don't let *you* tell you otherwise.

What we are is *a connection to* something. A connection to life. Connected. We are connected to God. God is in us. We are in God. Know your divinity. Declare it. **Te Deum. Divinus es.** Thou art God and *oh God* is that valuable!

God is existence, you exist, you are God's *expression*, you are like God: god-like. Being an expression of God is not too much to be. For a God which is existence, it is exactly what you should be, exactly what you are.

Welcome home.

The End

28. Endendum

What. is over. The book ended with Chapter 27. In earlier versions of this book, **Chapter 1, What We Are**, got *way* out of hand, *way* too long.

I decided to take it out of Chapter 1 and put it here on the end. For, like extra credit. Please don't feel you have to read this.

Here are six more tries to define us.

What We Are, Try #2: Connected to Soul

This try is difficult to grasp. Good luck with it.
It goes against everything everybody thinks about themselves.
It goes against what *you* think about *yourself.*
It goes against an idea that was taught to us as children.

Remember, just because we learned it when we were young doesn't mean it is true. It only means we believe it very deeply.
When they get you young, they get you *deep.*
We think deep ideas are true, just because they are deep.
Deep ideas are difficult to un-learn.
There's the deep difficult idea here. Ready?

We have separate brains.
My brain is not your brain.
My thoughts are not your thoughts.
So far, so good? Here's the hard part now.
We do not have separate souls.
My soul is your soul.
We think soul is inside us, as if our body could contain God.
Or is your god so small that it can fit in your body?

There is one light. There is only one light, one soul.
There is only one soul, the same soul for one and all.
Your soul is my soul.
We are all an expression of that one soul.
We are all an expression of life.
We do not have a soul. Soul has us.

We each *express* that one soul differently from anyone else.
But it's the same soul for everyone.
Same soul, different expression.

Because I am connected to that soul,
And you are connected to that soul,
And it's the same soul,
We are connected to each other.
Don't let your brain get in the way of your connections.

I recently heard the human-to-human connection called "empathic resonance." I really like the term. Does that help you understand it? It's not magic. It's not imaginary. It's real and we use it all the time. We just haven't quantified it yet. We will.

See? I told you it was difficult.

What we are:
We are a connection to soul.
Each and every one of us is a unique expression of God, of life, of soul.

What We Are, Try #3: Thinking

There is another way to look at us, to define us.
It has to do with thinking; what we think of ourselves.

A definition of "human being" is easy.

113

What are we?
We are what we think we are.
We are self-defined.
We improve ourselves by improving our thinking.
For better *and* worse, we are what we think we are.

Watch this.
What do we think we are?
Well, what *do* we think we are?

Are we Devil? Angel?
Sinner? Saint? Good? Bad?
Downtrodden? Uplifted?
Meat? Mind? Machine?
Hopeless? Hopeful?
Failed? Successful?
Smart? Stupid?
Fallen? Saved?

Yes! Yes! YES, we are! Any and all and more!
We *are* it if we think we are.

> The greatest revolution of our generation is the discovery that human beings,
> by changing the inner attitudes of their minds,
> can change the outer aspects of their lives.
> --William James

We do not need to raise ourselves up from the mud.
We do not dwell there. Except when we think we do.
And then we really *do* need to raise ourselves up from the mud.
And we can; and very often do.

There is no hell, except the hell that we create for ourselves.
Which is not to say there is no hell.
There is no devil, except for the things we are afraid of.
The devil is fear.
The devil is the thing(s) we are afraid of.

What Should We Think We Are

We are, at core, divine.
The expression of the light of life, remember?
Lift thinking to the understanding that we are divine, and in a while it becomes obvious. It took 45 years for me. Your mileage may vary. :-)

There is resistance to the idea that we just might be good, divine, wonderful creatures. Big resistance. *Huge* resistance. People seem to *need* the idea that we are condemned, worthless, stupid, and blundering our way towards extinction. It's a very popular idea.

Everybody has an inner voice that criticizes them.
Everybody thinks they are a dummy.
Everybody needs to be better informed about themselves.

It is not our weakness than needs strengthening, but our strength that needs controlling. We are not weak. Not by a long shot. Ten thousand years ago we banged rocks together to make fire. Today we bang subatomic particles together to make even smaller subatomic particles. We are not weak.

And we do one truly amazing thing. We determine reality.
Yes, we do.

We do that with a very simple technique: we decide the values of things. We decide that gold is valuable and dust is worthless. Nowhere but in our minds does it say that. From a million decisions we shape the world. We define the playing fields, the rules, the players, the score, and the importance of the game.

We determine reality!
Say that again, slowly: We. Determine. Reality.
We are beings of power.

We determine right and wrong.
Don't give that power to God. God gave that power to you.
We are divine. Nothing less.

But!
If we think we are weak, helpless, and stupid, then we are!
Simple as that.
Wouldn't you rather be strong and powerful?

What Is Reality?

So, now that I've used the word, what is this "reality" thing?
Especially if we determine it.

We think: "Reality is out there and I am in it. How it got there
I don't know, but there it is." I recently heard someone call reality "The Big Room."

We also think: "There is an '**I**,' a 'me' inside. I keep me hidden
and secret as much as I can." [36]

In other words, our rules of existence are:
- Reality: out there.
- Me: inside here.

So, what is this reality?
Here we go.

There is no barrier, no fence, no boundary between "out there,"
and "inside here."
Except that we think that there is.
Sometimes we *need* to think that there is.
But there isn't. *Out there* is solidly connected to *in here*.

The light shines through us.

---

[36] Maybe that's what "I" stands for: Inside.

We shine it out to the world in a billion ways, a trillion ways.
And in return everything else shines on us.
We're all shining on everything, and every thing is shining on us.
We're wired in. We're connected. We're on the grid. We're in the game, on the field.
We're in the Big Room.

Because of this, any definition of reality *must include us in it*.
We are part of the definition of reality. We are part of reality.

Once that is understood, we can see it's all one. No separation.

We pick and choose what we see. We ignore what we don't want to see. Or, as a Christian theologian once put it, "We find what we look for."[37]
We are *in* reality. Once that is fully understood, the answer to the question "What is reality?" is simple:
Reality is what we accept as real.
Reality is what you accept as real.

At every level we are defining reality all the time. We have our individual reality, our family's reality, our reality at work, our reality at play, our national reality…
The big mistake is thinking one size fits all. Not a chance.
Reality is relative; super relative. Your reality is *your* reality.

That's why it's so important to pray, attend services, learn the teachings of all the enlightened ones, the prophets, teachers, and from each other. Get other people's realities. Get realities from other points of view. Seek a wider understanding, and our reality will widen. That's why getting an education is important too. The better we think, the better our reality can be.

----

[37] That would be me. Henry David Thoreau said it too, just so's ya knows.

Think powerfully.

We are enormously powerful. We are so powerful; we can limit our power.
By thinking we are limited, we make it so. And keep it so.
We realize[38] ourselves into depression, poverty, addiction, war, disease, famine, and a billion other kinds of failure. We're good at it.

And yet we also do exactly the opposite. We realize[39] ourselves into wealth, happiness, economic boom, recovery, prosperity, health, and success in all fields. We're also good at that.

This is the sort of talking that keeps motivational speakers in business. It's still true. To lift ourselves up, lift up our thinking. There's no upper limit.

Don't blame the President. Don't blame the economy.
Don't blame anyone; don't give that power away.
It's us. We are powerful. We determine reality. Reality is what we accept as real.

Argue for your limitations, and sure enough they're yours. -Richard Bach

What We Are try #3 Summary

What are we?
We are what we think we are.

[38, 39.] "real-ize" Both mental and physical. To realize is to make real.

What We Are try #4: Communicating Creatures

Again, let me remind you that you don't have to be reading this chapter.

Come on back into the library again. There's one more good idea there.

The room is still dark. The sphere is hovering above the table. The light is still on inside it. The shapes are still shining on the walls like stars everywhere in the room.

Let's talk about talking

We are each a hole in the sphere. We are all holes in the sphere. When one of us communicates with another one of us, a connection between two holes on the sphere happens. An arc shoots up from one hole and comes down at another hole.

Imagine that. We connect together by talking.

Remember that we are not separate souls, but separate expressions of *the same* soul. **When one of us communicates with someone, what's really happening is life is connecting to itself.** Soul goes up and out through me, in through you, and back down to soul again.

This is a very big deal.

Your light combines with my light and produces a new light that has never existed before. This is communication. Life does this with us and it feels very good. We're a communicating species.

Life is always trying to express itself better and better.

That's why connection and communication are so universally popular and necessary.

What We Are try #4 Summary

What are we?
A connection to life, looking to connect to life.

What We Are try #5: A Law of the Universe!

Life must express itself as fully as possible. That seems to be a law of some kind. The history of the universe is the story of existence trying to express itself better and better. ·

And we've come a long, long way. We humans are the most subtle, beautiful, complex, full expression of existence so far attained.

We are the animals that ask.

We look upon ourselves and contemplate our own existence. "What am I?" "Who am I?" "Why am I?"
That is a really big deal.

What are we?
Getting better. **Nature wants better.** Here we are.

What We Are try #6: A Word from the Reaper

Remember, we're trying to define what we are.
Can't fully do that without a few words about death.

Everybody dies.
When we do, the connection to the light of life that we provided stops.

The light bulb at the center of the sphere is still on, but our hole is now closed.

When someone dies, we lose the connection to life that they provided us, the connection to life that they expressed, the connection to life that we connected through. We lose their connection.

But, by way of comfort, when someone dies, life still shines on. Look for it.

The light that they gave us still shines on us through other connections. Look for it.

What We Are try #7. A Connection To

We seem to be something, I mean, look in the mirror. There's something there, right? Here is where <u>what really is</u>, is different from <u>what seems to be</u>.

We are holes in a sphere, connected to life.
We are connections.
We aren't something by ourselves.
We're *a connection to* something.
Life is that something. That's what makes us something.
We are a connection to all of life.

You are not the light.
You are the window.
You don't have to be bright. You just have to be clear.

We don't stop at the skin.
We are not *in* our brains.
We are *through* our brains.

What We Are Summary

I told you right up front we are not what we seem to be.
I hope you can understand that now.

Humans are fascinating, complex, endearing, and worth know-ing. "They're my species."[40]

It takes more than a few words to adequately describe what we are. Sometimes those words are contradictory, a paradox.

We wouldn't want it any other way. Simple is boring.

- We are all expressions of life.
- We are enormously powerful.
- Our thinking determines our reality.
- We are participants in an ever-improving expression of life.
- We *are* something because we are *a connection to* some-thing.
- We communicate. The light through us connects to the light through others. Life connects to itself and expresses itself better.
- We carry the light of life.
- We are divine. Nothing less.

---

[40] *Harold and Maude*, written by Colin Higgins.

www.ingramcontent.com/pod-product-compliance
Lightning Source LLC
LaVergne TN
LVHW091224080426
835509LV00009B/1149